Passing the PCSO Recruit Assessment Process

Passing the PCSO Recruit Assessment Process

PETER COX

LawMatters
PUBLISHING

First published in 2007 by Law Matters Ltd.

British Library Cataloguing in Publication Data
A CIP record for this book is available from the British Library.

ISBN: 978 1 84641 059 8

Cover design by Code 5 Design Associates Ltd
Project management by Deer Park Productions
Typeset by Pantek Arts Ltd, Maidstone, Kent
Printed and bound in Great Britain by Cromwell Press Ltd, Trowbridge, Wiltshire

Law Matters Ltd
33 Southernhay East
Exeter EX1 1NX
Tel: 01392 215577
info@lawmatterspublishing.co.uk
www.lawmatterspublishing.co.uk

Contents

Acknowledgements

Peter Cox would like to thank his wife Janice for all the support, help and encouragement she gave him during his police career and while writing this book.

Every effort has been made to trace the copyright holders and to obtain their permission for the use of copyright material. The publisher and author will gladly receive information enabling them to rectify any error or omission in subsequent editions.

The author and publisher would like to thank the following for permission to reproduce copyright material: *The Integrated Competency Behavioural Framework – Version 9.0* (May 2007) reproduced in part in Appendix A of this book with the kind permission of Skills for Justice.

Chapter 1
Introduction

Why this book?

From 2002 Police Forces throughout England and Wales were able to recruit Police Community Support Officers. Their role was created to provide a high visibility uniformed presence within communities providing the reassurance communities said they wanted. Police Community Support Officers are within the community as a point of contact for members of the public and to work with the wider police service in preventing and detecting nuisance and low-level crime. In short their role is to focus on community safety issues thereby increasing the quality of life.

The role of Police Community Support Officer is a demanding one and some larger Police Forces have split the role into three specialist areas: -

• Transport

• Community

• Security

Whether general in nature or specialised, Police Community Support Officers wear a uniform and are required to work shifts, including evenings, weekends and bank holidays, during which time incidents may well involve conflict, and these can be challenging. It should also be considered that Police Community Support Officers are very often, after their initial training, required to patrol alone. All these issues should be considered in full before commencing the application process to become a Police Community Support Officer. The application process is demanding and time-consuming both for the candidate making the application and the police service who are to receive and process it.

Initially each individual police service designed and developed their own recruiting process for Police Community Support Officers however Central government were very keen to ensure criticisms levelled at the recruitment of Police Constables, prior to a national recruit process being introduced for them, were not repeated for the recruitment of Police Community Support Officers. Due to this a single process for the recruiting of Police Community Support Officers was introduced for individual police services to adopt from April 2006.

Advice and guidance available to people who are considering undergoing this assessment process are limited and vary in quality. This book, therefore, includes both an explanation of the national Police Community Support Officers Assessment Process and exercises that have been designed to help you acquire or enhance the skills and abilities you need to become a Police Community Support Officer.

You should work through the contents of this book in the order they are presented. This will assist you in understanding:

- the reasons why a national Police Community Support Officer Recruit Assessment Process has been established;

- the National Core Competencies;

- how to complete the written application;

- what is included in the assessment;

- the requirements for each section of the assessment;

- the skills and abilities required of a Police Community Support Officer (these are tested during the assessment process); and

- the feedback you receive following an assessment.

You should create a self-study plan when using this book. How you devise this and the detail it contains will be dictated by the time you have available prior to attending for your assessment however tasks for you to complete within this book will assist you to do this.

When you are preparing for the assessment process, you must obtain certain information and guidance. This will help you when you come to consider and develop your skills and abilities. It is important that you obtain information and guidance from more than one person: detailed feedback from a number of different sources will enable you to assess yourself accurately and will help you to develop the appropriate skills. Try, therefore, to get help from at least three different people, preferably from different walks of life (for example, from your family, work and social environments). You should also read – and make sure you understand – the information your local service sends you prior to attending for assessment.

A number of issues are mentioned on more than one occasion in this book. This will help you to understand the requirements for that particular part of the assessment process and will also reinforce the key learning points.

Background to the national Police Community Support Officers Recruit Assessment Process

Before the national Police Community Support Officers Recruit Assessment Process was established, each police force in England and Wales was responsible for its own recruiting methods. This led to variations in the skills and abilities that were being assessed, and to what standards. In addition, the actual assessment of individual candidates varied a great deal. It was for these reasons, and to prevent criticisms previously made of recruiting into the police service, that a nationally recognised, robust and standardised procedure was proposed. The result was the National Police Community Support Officers Recruit Assessment Process, which was designed and implemented by the national police training organisation, Centrex (now superseded by the National Policing Improvement Agency).

As part of this process, 'Assessment Centres' were created. Even though the term 'Assessment Centre' suggests otherwise, an Assessment Centre is really a process rather than a building or a place. For a recruiting process to be considered an Assessment Centre, certain key elements must be present. These are:

- The candidates' skills and abilities are tested a number of different times.

- These skills and abilities are tested through different exercises and the interview questions.

- The assessments that arise from these exercises and the interview are used to produce the final results.

- A number of assessors are used throughout the process.

- These assessors must have the appropriate training before they are permitted to assess.

- Candidates are provided with feedback on their performance following assessment.

Using different exercises, an interview and a number of trained assessors ensures fairness and equality for all. Candidates are therefore given a range of opportunities to display the skills necessary to become a Police Community Support Officer.

If a traditional recruitment interview was used as the only method of selection, this would suit some candidates more than others. For example, if a candidate started the interview badly, it would be very difficult for him or her to recover, causing the candidate to feel that he or she was unable to show his or her real abilities. At an Assessment Centre, however, candidates move quickly from one exercise or interview question to the next. It is therefore important not to dwell on what has just happened but to focus on what comes next.

Approximately five assessors contribute to the assessment of each individual candidate. These people are not given any information about the candidates they are to assess. In addition, they are unable to communicate with the other assessors before they begin or complete their assessments. This ensures that, at each stage of the process, a candidate is starting with a clean slate as far as that particular assessor is concerned.

It is thus generally accepted that Assessment Centres are more reliable in recruiting appropriate people when compared with single-form recruiting methods, such as traditional interviews. It is for this reason that, within the police service, Assessment Centres are used not only for recruitment purposes but also for promotion.

Assessment Centre exercises

Each set of exercises takes approximately six months to design and develop before it reaches an appropriate standard whereby it can be used to assess candidates. This design process follows nationally agreed standards and has various phases. These include:

- research

- design

- development

- trials

- review

- refinement.

Many exercises are discarded at different stages of the design process if they are shown to contain any weaknesses or flaws. Those that are selected must demonstrate in each phase that they will assess candidates consistently and fairly.

Those involved in the design process include occupational psychologists, people trained in recruitment processes and lay people representing a wide cross-section of the community. In total, up to 500 people will be involved, at some stage, in the design process.

How candidates are assessed

Clusters of skills and abilities are assessed during each exercise and the interview. These are called the National Core Competencies, which are discussed in the next chapter. At the conclusion of the assessment process, the same competency areas from each of the exercises are added together. This means that, if the competency area Community and Customer Focus is considered in three exercises, the scores for these three exercises will be added together, resulting in a total score for the area of Community and Customer Focus. In this way a candidate will not fail the entire assessment simply because he or she has performed badly in one particular exercise. Candidates are thus given every opportunity to demonstrate their skills and abilities and to achieve an assessment that reflects those skills and abilities.

There is one exception to this: the area of Respect for Race and Diversity. Should a candidate display behaviour that is totally inappropriate for the conduct of a Police Community Support Officer, then that candidate will be considered unsuitable, no matter how good his or her other skills and abilities are, or how well he or she performs in this competency area in other exercises. The reason for this is simple: when a Police Community Support Officer deals with the public, if he or she behaves badly, it does not matter how well he or she resolves the issue, the public's perception of the police service is likely to be poor. This will probably remain so even if all their other interactions with the police service are favourable. (The area of Respect for Race and Diversity is explained in more detail in **Chapter 8**.)

The required standard

The required standard of performance is the same for all candidates, but it is altered from time to time for a variety of reasons. It will, however, usually require the candidates to achieve a minimum of approximately 50 per cent of the total score available to be successful. All candidates' scores are judged against a preset standard – candidates are not judged against one another.

When a candidate has completed an assessment, his or her scores for each exercise, and for each competency area, are added together. These scores are combined with the scores from the other areas to arrive at the final mark. The minimum set score must be achieved to be successful. This scoring system allows candidates to be below the set level in one particular area (such as community and customer focus) but to be above the minimum in another skills set. The set minimum, however, must be achieved in the area of Respect for Race and Diversity and in a candidate's written communications because these are considered critical to being an effective Police Community Support Officer.

Assessors

The assessors used at Assessment Centres come from all walks of life, including the police service. While some people say that only police service employees should be allowed to assess, it can also be argued that the community in general should contribute to selecting those people who will be entrusted to work with them in upholding law and order and adding to their quality of life.

Before they are allowed to assess, the assessors must undergo training. This training includes role acting because assessors are required to role act during the interactive exercises. In addition to this initial training, prior to any Assessment Centre commencing, assessors are trained in the exercise that they will operate for the duration of that Assessment Centre. Before they begin to assess and during the time they are assessing they are tested to ensure the appropriate high standards are maintained from the beginning of the assessment right through to its conclusion.

The Assessment Centre management team

In addition to trained assessors, each Assessment Centre has a designated management team. These people have the responsibility for setting up and administrating the Assessment Centre and for ensuring that all policies, procedures and guidelines are followed correctly. Depending on the number of candidates to be assessed each day, this team usually comprises of six people.

Management team members will have been trained appropriately and they constantly monitor the exercises and tests to see that they are working correctly. This ensures that every candidate, from the first to the last, gets the same opportunity to display his or her skills and abilities.

General assumptions

Throughout the book you will find 'General assumption' boxes. These boxes contain the preconceived ideas many candidates have prior to their attending an Assessment Centre. These ideas often originate from candidates who have previously attended an Assessment Centre or from unofficial websites. Many of these assumptions are wrong, misleading or incomplete.

These boxes not only highlight what is generally assumed about Assessment Centres but also list the facts of the situation. An example is as follows:

GENERAL ASSUMPTION

If you perform very badly in one exercise you will fail the Assessment Centre.

FACT

This is not the case. In each exercise a number of skill areas will be assessed. These are added to the scores for the same skill areas when these areas are assessed during other exercises or tests. All the scores from each exercise are then added together. It is the overall score that is important, not the score achieved in any particular exercise. As mentioned above, the only exception to this is the area of Respect for Race and Diversity and a candidate's written communications.

If you have any preconceived ideas about Assessment Centres, it is worth checking to see if these are accurate: this book will assist you in this.

Tasks

This book contains tasks for you to consider and complete. Some have been designed to demonstrate the types of exercises you will meet during the assessment. If you familiarise yourself with the exercise types now, during your assessment you will be able to concentrate on displaying the appropriate skills and abilities rather than being concerned with the mechanics of the process.

Other tasks ask you to consider the current level of your skills and abilities against those required to be a Police Community Support Officer, and to consider how these can be monitored and developed before you attend for an assessment. It is important that you view these tasks as a way of gaining the skills necessary to be an efficient and effective Police Community Support Officer, not as tricks or as a way to pass at an Assessment Centre. The more time you devote to these tasks before you attend the Assessment Centre, the greater will be your chances of demonstrating your true skills and abilities when you do attend.

GENERAL ASSUMPTION

You can be trained to pass an Assessment Centre.

FACT

You can be trained so that you understand how the Assessment Centre operates, and this training will make you more comfortable during the process. Equally, you can be trained in the skills and abilities (called competencies) that will be tested during an assessment. To be successful, you should develop your skills and abilities rather than train in a system for passing the assessment centre.

Top tips

All chapters close with a 'top tips' box. These can be used as a refresher or as a revision aid. They should help you to reinforce the key learning points for each chapter. If there is anything in a top-tips box you do not understand, reread the relevant parts of that chapter. Space has been provided after each top-tips box so that you can add your own individual learning points for referring to at a later date.

The top-tips boxes look as follows:

TOP TIPS

- Before applying consider fully the role a Police Community Support Officer has to perform. Remember you will be required to work shifts and weekends.

- Devise and follow a self-study plan.

- Use more than one source of information when preparing for the Assessment Centre.

- Always read the information you receive from the police service to which you have applied regarding the Assessment Centre.

- When completing an exercise at the Assessment Centre, do not reflect on what you have just done – concentrate on what comes next.

- Remember, you are in competition with the Assessment Centre standards, not with other candidates.

- Use the 'assumption boxes' to help you consider your own preconceived ideas.

- Look to develop skills and abilities necessary to be a Police Community Support Officer rather than skills and abilities to pass at the Assessment Centre.

- Use the top tips to reinforce the key learning points.

- Record any personal learning from the chapter under the heading 'Individual learning points'.

INDIVIDUAL LEARNING POINTS

_____

_____

_____

_____

_____

_____

_____

_____

Chapter 2
The National Core Competencies

Introduction

The National Core Competencies are a list of indicators that describe the attributes necessary, across a range of skills and abilities, to become a Police Community Support Officer. They simply describe the attitudes and behaviours that are required during every-day interactions.

During the assessment, six core competencies are assessed:

(a) Respect for Race and Diversity.

(b) Team Working.

(c) Community and Customer Focus.

(d) Effective Communication.

(e) Personal Responsibility.

(f) Resilience.

Each competency area comprises of a title, a description (in sentence form) of what the area means and a further statement describing the required standard for that competency. Below each area is a list of positive and negative indicators. These describe the types of attitudes and behaviours that should be used by Police Community Support Officers. (**Appendix A** contains a full list of the National Core Competencies taken from Skills for Justice *Integrated Competency Behavioural Framework – Version 9.0*, but do not read this until you have completed Task 1 in this chapter.)

When you look at the list of National Core Competencies, you will see that there are many different ways you can demonstrate these indicators during an assessment. **Chapter 5** contains a sample interactive exercise assessment checklist, and this demonstrates how behaviours are assessed and linked to the competencies. Occasionally, the words used within the headings or descriptions are amended but, if this happens, it is unlikely that the skills you are required to demonstrate during an assessment will have changed.

Which competencies are assessed in which exercises

You will not know which competencies are being assessed in the interactive and written exercises, but each competency will be assessed a minimum of three times. Remember that Respect for Race and Diversity is assessed throughout the entire process and that your oral communication skills are assessed during all interactive exercises and during the interview.

With the exception of the interview, you should not concern yourself with which of the competencies is being assessed: focus on what is in front of you. During the interview, on the other hand, you will be told which competency area is being assessed in each question, so your answers should focus on the required abilities within that area.

Develop the required skills prior to attending for assessment and then apply those skills accordingly. Refining these skills and abilities is the key to a successful career, as it is these skills and abilities that are developed during training and are monitored and reported on in annual appraisals.

GENERAL ASSUMPTION

The interview during the assessment centre carries more weight in terms of marking than other parts of the assessment centre.

FACT

Each of the interview questions only cover one competency area, although Oral Communication and Respect for Race and Diversity will be considered throughout the interview. The scores from each interview question are added to the appropriate competency area scores from each of the other exercises. As such no one area of the assessment centre is more important than another.

Using the competencies to prepare for an assessment

Before you attend for an assessment, you should use the positive and negative indicators to help you to prepare by:

- Identifying the key requirements for each of the competency areas.

- Reviewing your current skills level against the competencies.

- Developing your positive traits.

- Ridding yourself of, or amending, your negative behaviours.

Developing your skills against the competencies

A systematic way to develop your skills and abilities is to undertake the following tasks:

- Review what competencies are required.

- Assess your current skill levels.

- Develop and implement action plans for those areas where you are not achieving the competency requirements and to improve your overall performance.

TASK 1

Reviewing what skills and abilities are required

Listed below are the headings for each competency area. These are followed by sentences that explain what the areas are about. Below this is a statement describing the required standard for each competency area. Finally, there are spaces in the boxes with the headings 'positive traits' and 'negative traits' in the corner.

To work out what skills and abilities are required to be a Police Community Support Officer, read each competency heading, the sentence that explains what the area is about and the statement outlining the required standard.

In the positive traits boxes, list what you believe would be the skills and abilities required for that competency area. Similarly list what you believe would be the negative traits. To assist you with this, a few example traits have been given for the area of Respect for Race and Diversity. You should try to record approximately ten traits for each area.

Respect for Race and Diversity
A Police Community Support Officer:
Considers and shows respect for the opinions, circumstances and feelings of colleagues and members of the public, no matter what their race, religion, position, background, circumstances, status or appearance.

Required standard
A Police Community Support Officer:
Understands other people's views and takes them into account.
Is tactful and diplomatic when dealing with people.
Treats people with dignity and respect at all times.
Understands, and is sensitive to, social, cultural and racial differences.

Positive traits	*Negative traits*
Understanding other people's views	*Not taking into account other*
Speaking correctly to the public	*people's needs*
Not breaking confidences	*Using offensive language*
	Telling inappropriate jokes

TASK 1

Team Working

A Police Community Support Officer:

Develops strong working relationships inside and outside the team to achieve common goals.

Breaks down barriers between groups and involves others in discussion and decisions.

Required standard

A Police Community Support Officer:

Works effectively as a team member and helps build relationships within the team.

Actively helps and supports others to achieve team goals.

Positive traits	*Negative traits*

Community and Customer Focus

A Police Community Support Officer:

Focuses on the customer and provides a high-quality service that is tailored to meet their individual needs.

Understands the communities that are served and shows an active commitment to policing that reflects their needs and concerns.

Required standard

A Police Community Support Officer:

Provides a high level of service to customers.

Maintains contact with customers, works out what they need and responds to them.

Positive traits	*Negative traits*

TASK 1

Effective Communication
A Police Community Support Officer:
Communicates ideas and information effectively, both verbally and in writing.
Uses language and a style of communication that is appropriate to the situation and people being addressed.
Makes sure that others understand what is going on.

Required standard
A Police Community Support Officer:
Speaks clearly and concisely, and does not use jargon.
Uses plain English and correct grammar.
Listens carefully to understand.

Positive traits	*Negative traits*

Personal Responsibility
A Police Community Support Officer:
Takes personal responsibility for making things happen and achieving results.
Displays motivation, commitment, perseverance and conscientiousness.
Acts with a high degree of integrity.

Required standard
A Police Community Support Officer:
Takes personal responsibility for own actions and for sorting out issues or problems that arise.
Is focused on achieving results to required standards and developing skills and knowledge.

Positive traits	*Negative traits*

TASK 1

Resilience
A Police Community Support Officer:
Shows resilience, even in difficult circumstances.
Is prepared to make difficult decisions and has the confidence to see them through.

Required standard
A Police Community Support Officer:
Shows confidence to perform own role without unnecessary support in normal circumstances.
Acts in an appropriate way and controls emotions.

Positive traits	*Negative traits*

When you have done this for each competency, compare your list with the National Core Competencies in **Appendix A**. Remember to read the positive and negative indicators in the context of the descriptive sentence and the outline of the required standard.

The words you will have used may not be the same as those listed in the National Core Competencies. When making the comparison, however, what is important is the meaning rather than the specific words. You should make a note of where you have missed a behaviour or attitude, or where you have considered something as positive when it should be assessed as negative, and vice versa.

Highlight the discrepancies between your own and the national list. This will develop your understanding of each competency area and of the skills and abilities contained within it. Reread the competencies a number of times and on different occasions to make sure you understand them. It is important to understand the skills and abilities that are required in a modern police service. Behaviours and attitudes often displayed on police television programmes are very often not the skills that are required or expected.

GENERAL ASSUMPTION

The competency area Respect for Race and Diversity applies only to issues of sexuality and race.

FACT

Respect for Race and Diversity does indeed relate to these issues, and they are important in modern policing, but they apply equally well to all differences in society. These differences are many and varied and may not always be immediately obvious.

For example, a group of youths aged between 10 and 14 years are playing outside a retired persons' complex to the annoyance of the residents. The difference is the age range of the two groups, and this difference may affect each group's understanding of the situation. A key element of policing is to appreciate that different groups of people have different understandings of what is going on and why it is going on. Dealing with contrasting views – without taking sides – requires understanding and sensitivity.

During the assessment you should demonstrate that you have considered and understand both viewpoints before deciding on a course of action. It is important that you base your decisions on facts and not on assumptions. Do not, for instance, assume that the youths must be in the wrong.

TASK 2

Assessing your skills against the requirements

Once you understand each of the competency areas, you should consider your current skills level within each. Take time to reflect on your skills and abilities and compare these honestly with the national standards. Use the competencies listed in **Appendix B** to record an outline of your own abilities. Each area in **Appendix B** has been separated into strengths and areas for development.

Avoid generalisations and try to be as specific as possible: think about the way you behave and speak and the attitudes you display. If it helps, consider specific incidents you have been involved in and how you assisted in resolving them. Another way to do this is to monitor yourself, noting any common themes in your behaviour or actions.

An example of how you could complete **Appendix B** is given below:

Effective Communication
Strengths *I listen to what I am being told* *I check what I have been told by asking questions* *I use different words to take into account the different people I'm speaking to (i.e. children)* *Areas for development* *I am sometimes nervous when speaking to people I do not know* *I say things without thinking through the consequences* *I can ramble when talking*

When you have completed the task, compare your strengths and areas for development with those listed in **Appendix A**. Make sure you listed things under the correct headings. For example, the following may have been listed as a strength: 'To reinforce my speech, I talk over other people to make sure I'm heard.' You may think this falls under a positive heading (i.e. make sure communication has a clear purpose). However in most circumstances this would be considered a negative trait, and is listed in the indicators as 'does not listen and interrupts at inappropriate times'.

Having reflected on and recorded your own level of performance, confirm your results by obtaining feedback from family, friends or work colleagues. Select people you believe can make the most accurate judgements about you. Although it is tempting to choose only those people who, you believe, will give you positive feedback, this will not assist you in identifying areas for development.

Use the six competency headings to help these people focus on your different skills and abilities. This will give direction to their feedback. You could also look at any appraisals you may have had in your current employment. If you do this, however, you should make sure that what is considered positive or negative in your current work would also be regarded so within a policing environment.

When you seek feedback from people, ask them to be honest and open. Should the feedback be unclear, ask them to expand their thoughts and to give precise examples where possible. This will help to confirm that the feedback is appropriate and will therefore assist you in your understanding.

For example, a friend says to you: 'Sometimes you are a bit unclear.' Try to establish exactly what he or she means:

- Do you mumble?

- Does your voice trail off towards the end of sentences?

- Are your sentences sometimes confused?

- On occasions, do you change the direction of a conversation mid-sentence?

- Or do you use wrong or inappropriate words?

The clearer the feedback, the easier it is to work out how you can change your behaviour. Ask these people to give you examples of what you said and did. Even though it is difficult to listen to adverse comments about yourself, avoid becoming defensive and accept what you are being told. Try to decide how accurate the feedback is: compare it with your own assessment of yourself and with that of others. Come to terms with the fact that other people's perceptions of your behaviour may not be the same as your own.

At times feedback from different sources will contradict. Look for common themes that accord with your own evaluation of your abilities. In this way you should identify appropriate areas and clear targets for development.

TASK 3

Action planning to improve your performance

Having completed an evaluation of your skills and abilities and having obtained feedback from others, you should now have a clear understanding of what you do well. Continue to develop these positive skills and abilities so that your confidence increases.

You should also have gained an insight into those attitudes and abilities that require development. It's a good idea to list these to make them clear. When you have done

> this, grade each item in order of priority, starting with the area that received the most negative feedback.
>
> **You should now devise an action plan for each item on the list. An action plan is simply a written set of instructions to help you focus on what it is you need to do or improve, what you need to achieve and a time frame in which to do it.**

Action plans

Police Community Support Officers are often given developmental action plans during their training using SMART objectives. These usually contain the following words:

- 'Specific': an outline of those *specific* things that need to be developed or improved. This should be listed as a positive attitude or behaviour, not a negative one. For example, you realise you must allow others to stop speaking before you reply, rather than talking over them. This section of the plan should contain an outline of how you are to go about this, perhaps in the form of simple steps you intend to take to achieve the required development.

- 'Measurable': the ways the improvement or development can be *measured*.

- 'Relevant' and 'Achievable': the actions you intend to take are *relevant* in that they will actually *achieve* the required development. The action plan may not contain these words, but they will help you to consider whether the steps you are taking will bring about the required learning.

- 'Timescale': the *timescale* within which the required development can be achieved and measured should be realistic.

Obviously, the time you have available prior to attending an Assessment Centre will dictate the number and depth of any action plans you devise.

Below is an example of an action plan for a candidate who has identified that he or she often interrupts others without good reason.

Example action plan

Specific: you must allow others to finish speaking before you reply. This will be achieved by completing the following actions:

- Identifying those who can assist you with this action plan.

- Informing those people of your proposed plan and seeking their agreement to assist you in this.

- Asking them to inform you when you fail to allow others to finish speaking.

- Asking them, when appropriate, to stop you when you begin to talk before others have finished.

- Agreeing how and when they will give you feedback.

- Continuing to receive feedback until you can demonstrate that the action plan has been achieved.

Measurable: ask family, friends and work colleagues to note down when you interrupt others. Ask them to continue with this feedback even when you no longer talk over others (i.e. their feedback will be a measure of your success in your action plan).

Achievable: for your plan to be considered successful, under normal circumstances, in the majority of occasions you allow others to finish speaking before you reply.

Timescale: you will be monitored over a two-week period, during which time the circumstances and occasions when this happens will be identified. At the end of this period, you should be able to assess whether or not the action plan has been successful. If it has, no further plans for this developmental area are required, other than ongoing monitoring. For more complex plans, a timescale should be set for each individual action.

The number of action plans to be used

For each developmental area you have identified, write an action plan. It is, however, advisable to use no more than three at any one time. If you use more than three, the feedback you receive from others and your own self-monitoring may become generalised or unclear.

When you have completed an action plan, introduce a new one until all your developmental areas have been covered. However, continue to monitor your developmental areas even after an action plan has been completed – this should prevent old patterns of behaviour from returning.

TOP TIPS

- Identify each of the National Core Competencies areas.

- Identify appropriate positive and negative traits for each competency area.

- Identify and correct any misunderstandings regarding the competency requirements.

- Review your personal strengths and development areas against the National Core Competencies.

- Ask for feedback from family, friends and work colleagues.

- Using the National Core Competencies, identify your own personal development areas.

- Create action plans for your developmental needs.

- Prioritise your action plans.

- Write action plans using the 'SMART' method

- Activate your action plans in order of priority.

- Remember that the competency area Respect for Race and Diversity is assessed throughout the entire process.

INDIVIDUAL LEARNING POINTS

Chapter 3
The Application Form

Introduction

(*Note*: If possible, have a copy of the application form next to you when reading this chapter.)

Before you can attend an Assessment Centre, you must fill in an application form and submit this to the police force of your choice. This application form has four sections:

(a) Information about yourself.

(b) Your employment history.

(c) Your education and skills.

(d) A competency assessment.

First of all, read the guidance notes on the application form before you answer any of the questions. Then, *using a piece of scrap paper*, write down exactly what you intend to put on the form, particularly in the competency assessment section. Now ask someone to read what you have written and, if necessary, to correct your spelling and grammar – you do not want your application to be rejected simply because it contains spelling and grammatical mistakes.

When you are happy with the wording, make a few photocopies of the form – again, *before* you fill it in. You can then use these copies to practise filling in the actual form. This should prevent you from making mistakes. In the competency assessment section, for example, there is only a limited amount of space for you to write your evidence. Practise filling this in: you want to provide clear evidence but not cram so many words into the box that your writing becomes illegible.

Look at the information provided at the start of each section on the form. This states clearly that, if you are not completing the form online, you should complete it in black ink. Make sure you do, and make sure the pen you intend to use has sufficient ink to fill in the entire form – a change of pen halfway through an application form looks unsightly.

Section 1: About you

All applicants are vetted to make sure they are suitable to join the police service. It is for this reason that you should complete the section regarding convictions and cautions openly and honestly. Declare all your convictions and cautions and any that may be pending – even those for motoring offences. The force you have applied to will check your form with various police databases. If you have omitted something, this will result in your application being rejected. If you are uncertain as to whether a certain conviction may bar you from applying, contact the force's recruiting department for clarification. After all, you do not want to waste your time and effort completing the application form only to find out you are ineligible.

Similar inquiries will be made about your close family and associates, and this is why it is essential you complete the section 'About your family' accurately.

Section 2: About your employment

As with the other sections, make sure you leave yourself sufficient space to provide all the information requested. For example, the column headed 'Reason for leaving/wanting to leave' does not allow you much room for your answer. Practise filling this in on one of your photocopies. In the section about your previous employment, start with your most recent job. If you run out of space to list all your previous employment, continue on a separate sheet.

In the section headed 'Referees', ideally you should put your current or previous employer. If you have never been employed, you can provide personal references (for example, if you have been involved in voluntary work). If you are a member of Her Majesty's armed forces, you will need to provide a covering letter outlining the date or projected date of your discharge.

Section 3: About your education and skills

You do not need any formal educational qualifications, specific skills or particular experiences to apply to be a police community support officer. When completing this section, again, start with your most recent qualifications and work backwards. Do not cram all the details into the limited space provided: you are allowed to continue on a separate sheet.

Section 4: Competency assessment

This is the most important part of the form because you will be assessed against the information you provide. You will not progress to the next stage of the selection process if you do not provide evidence of your competency in this section.

As a reminder, the National Core Competencies are as follows:

- Respect for Race and Diversity.
- Team Working.
- Community and Customer Focus.
- Effective Communication.
- Personal Responsibility.
- Resilience.

An assessor will use a checklist to score you on this section. To be successful, you must attain a set minimum score. A number of marks are available for each of the three questions, and you must provide evidence for all of them. It is not, therefore, good enough to mark an answer with a comment similar to 'I have no experience in this area and so I am unable to answer the question'.

It is vital you write neatly in this section – if the assessor cannot read your answer, how can he or she score it? Also be careful with your spelling, grammar and punctuation. Practising on the photocopies will pay dividends in this section: you are not allowed to use continuation sheets and any writing outside the space provided will not be marked.

You can use examples from your private, work or educational life. This should give you ample opportunities to answer the questions. However, read the *entire* question before you answer, not just the broad title above it. Once you have read the question, think of a number of events/incidents/situations you feel would provide you with a suitable answer. Make notes on each and consider whether the event/incident/situation would provide you with adequate information to answer the question comprehensively.

When you have read the main question that asks you to recall a situation, consider the sub-questions. These ask for further details. Write these in the boxes provided. Remember, only complete the actual application form after a friend or relative has checked your draft answer for content, spelling, punctuation and grammar. The following is an example of how a situation can be used to provide evidence for this section of the form.

Michael is a 21-year-old student studying for a degree in geography. His course will end in the next three months. He is at the stage of his degree course that involves a number of field trips. Consequently, he has to work not only as part of a team but also on his own. He is a member of his local rugby club and regularly plays on a Saturday afternoon. To help fund his degree course, he has a part-time job in a local supermarket stacking shelves. He works shifts but he makes sure they do not interfere with his university work.

Michael can draw on events/incidents/situations that have occurred during his degree course, sporting activities and part-time job. Therefore, if a question on the application form was worded as follows he would be able to draw on all three activities:

It is vitally important that police community support officers work as part of a team. Please recall an example when you have worked as part of a team and your contribution ensured that the team met its goals or targets.

Describe the situation

I was working late one evening in the supermarket when a couple of people rang in to say they were too ill to attend work. This resulted in the team of shelf stackers being short staffed. We were expecting a large delivery that had to be unloaded quickly as the lorry had other stores to attend. The warehouse staff would unload the lorry but it was our responsibility to have the goods displayed on the relevant shelves before the store closed for the night.

What exactly did you do in the situation described?

I suggested to the other shelf stackers that we divide the store into areas. This would mean we would not waste time moving around the store – time that would be better spent stacking the shelves. We would then have a better chance to complete the job before the store closed. They agreed this was the best way to tackle the problem. I then suggested that we have a look to see exactly what had been delivered and then decide which areas of the store required our attention. Once we had examined the delivery and were aware of the aisles where the goods had to be stacked, I allocated each one of us an area of the store.

What was the result of your actions?

Although it was hard work we got the goods to the correct aisles and shelves in the time we had available to us. This meant the store was ready for opening the following day. The store manager thanked us all for our efforts. She particularly thanked me for organising the team. Since this occurred we now follow the same method with every delivery.

What do you think the consequences would have been if you had not acted in the way described?

The shelves would not have been stacked in time for the store closing. This would have resulted in someone having to do the work when he or she arrived the following morning. This would have had an effect on our team's reputation. The store may not have been ready for customers arriving, which would also have had an effect on the store's reputation. If customers could not buy the goods they wanted on this occasion they might consider doing their shopping elsewhere.

In this example the applicant has used an incident from his work experience to good effect in answering the questions posed. He has read the questions and answered each in a brief but informative manner.

Additional questions

In addition to the competency questions there are two further questions, these are:

1. Why do you want to be a police community support officer?

2. What tasks you would expect to do as a police community support officer?

When answering the first of these questions answer it honestly, but consider why police community support officers were introduced. At this stage it may be worth rereading the opening paragraphs on page 1. In essence the role can be considered very similar to an old style 'bobby on the beat', working with and providing reassurance to the community.

When answering the second question look at the information provided by the force to which you have applied. This will very often include a list of key tasks you will be expected to perform if selected. In addition to this many police forces web sites have accounts and experiences from the working lives of current police community support officers. Use this information to form a clear and accurate picture of the tasks a police community support officer does on a daily basis.

TOP TIPS

- Double check your spelling and grammar.
- Photocopy the application form a number of times.
- Read the question and sub-questions carefully then formulate your answer.
- Practise writing your answer to ensure it fits into the space provided on the application form.
- Make sure your answer is legible. If the assessor cannot read it you will not be rewarded for your answer.
- Use examples from your personal, work or private life.
- Before answering the additional questions carry out appropriate research.
- Have another person check your application form.

INDIVIDUAL LEARNING POINTS

_____

_____

_____

_____

_____

_____

_____

_____

_____

Chapter 4
Assessment Centres

Introduction

Police Forces were required to adopt the National Police Community Support Officers Assessment Centre from April 2006. Forces will move to this process as they receive appropriate training and put in place the required infrastructure to support it. If you are uncertain, check with the Force to which you have applied that they have adopted the national process. Even if that is not the case the contents of this book will help you prepare by considering and developing the skills that will be assessed no matter what the content of the recruiting process. It will also demonstrate the types or exercises that can be and are used by the police when recruiting or selecting for promotion.

This chapter considers Assessment Centres and suggests some do's and don'ts about the centres that should ensure you avoid any pitfalls and understand what is expected of you.

It is not unusual to feel ill at ease in such situations as this, and you will not be the only person who is feeling nervous. However, take heart from the fact that the Assessment Centre has been designed to allow you to demonstrate your skills and abilities in full, not to catch you out. One of the strengths of an Assessment Centre is that it is a clear and transparent process: there are no tricks or hidden agendas.

Exercises and tests

During your assessment through the National process, you will be expected to complete the following:

- Two interactive exercises.

- Two written exercises.

- An interview comprising four questions.

The order in which you will be asked to complete the exercises and tests will be given to you on the day. A set time is allowed for each exercise and test.

Interactive and written exercises

When you are completing these, you will be asked to fulfil a job role in a named organisation. As an example and for the purposes of this book you will be a 'Mobile First Contact Support Officer' in a National Health Trust when completing tasks for the written and interactive exercises.

The job role you are given and the organisation are always fictitious. This is to ensure that all candidates are given the same opportunity. You will be provided with a full outline of the job role and its responsibilities. In addition, you will be given background information regarding the organisation and its policies that may be of benefit to you.

Once you are familiar with the role and the exercises, you will see that they are very similar to the role of a Police Community Support Officer and to the situations and tasks they are required to deal with.

Throughout the assessment process, no legal knowledge or police experience is required or expected.

Interviews

For the interview you are expected to be yourself. When questioned regarding your previous experiences, you can use examples from your work, education or leisure activities. As the assessors have no prior knowledge of the candidates, if appropriate, you can use the answers you gave to the questions during the written application stage.

GENERAL ASSUMPTION

When answering interview questions answers giving examples of police experience score higher than other answers.

FACT

Each answer given by a candidate is marked against a predefined assessment sheet. This assessment sheet will reflect the positive traits for the competency area to which the question relates. Whether the answer given by the candidate is police related or not will not affect how it is scored by the assessor.

What you will receive before you attend

You will be notified in writing of the date, time and location of your Assessment Centre. In addition, you will be sent two documents:

- A brief explanation of the Assessment Centre.

- The background information and job role you are required to fulfil when completing the written and interactive exercises.

You will be sent these documents at least two weeks before you attend for assessment. You will be asked before the assessment begins if you have received these documents.

If not, you will be asked if you want to continue with the assessment or whether you want to be rescheduled until you have had the time to receive and digest the information.

Remember that some forces may only hold Assessment Centres one week in every six months, depending on their recruiting requirements. If this is the case for the force you have applied to, it could delay your application for a considerable time. If you have not received the full information but decide to go ahead anyway, should you not be successful, you will not be allowed to appeal on these grounds. If you have been preparing in advance of your receiving this material (e.g. by getting the documents from the web or other sources), it is important that you check to see whether any alterations have been made when the material arrives.

While all the information provided in the background information on the job role will not be used during the Assessment Centre, you will not know in advance which parts are to be used. Knowing all the information prior to attending will help you understand the role you are required to perform during the interactive and written exercises, and the standards expected from you.

Check the time, date and location of the Assessment Centre. The assessment will start at the stated time and, if you arrive once it has commenced, you may be unable to take part. If this happens you will have to wait for a future appointment. As mentioned above, if you miss your allotted slot you may have to wait a lengthy period of time for another appointment.

The information you are sent will list the documents you should take with you as evidence of your identity. Make sure you take these with you – failure to do so may prevent you from taking part. These documents include a full 10-year passport or two of the following:

- A British driving licence.
- A P45.
- A birth certificate issued within six weeks of your birth.
- A cheque book and bank card with three statements and proof of signature.
- A credit card containing a photograph of yourself.
- Proof of residence (e.g. a council tax or utility bill).

Illness

Whether the Assessment Centre is operated by an individual police service or a group of services, it represents a large investment in terms of money and resources. Should you become ill prior to attending for an assessment, it is very important that you contact the service to which you have applied as soon as possible. This will give the service the opportunity to fill the space created by your non-attendance.

Before the assessment begins, you will be asked if you are fit and well. If you feel ill, this is the time to say, so that your Assessment Centre can be rescheduled. If you commence the assessment but have to withdraw, this will normally be classed as your being unsuccessful.

Candidates with specific needs

If you have a physical disability, you should talk directly to the police service to which you have applied regarding what is, or is not, considered to be a bar to service. If you have a temporary disability, you should still speak to the service to which you have applied about the nature of your disability and the restrictions this may cause in terms of preventing you from performing to the best of your abilities during the assessment. Every effort will be made to change either the physical location or the structure of the Assessment Centre to ensure fairness to all candidates.

Should you have a specific learning disability, such as dyslexia, this will be taken into account during the assessment. For this to happen, however, you should inform the relevant police service. They will ask you to submit a report outlining your learning difficulty. This report should be completed by a specialist in adult learning difficulties.

This report is studied by a psychologist who will make recommendations, if appropriate, for changes to the structure of the Assessment Centre. An example of such an adjustment for a candidate with dyslexia would be for him or her to be awarded an extra 25 per cent preparation time for the written exercises and for the preparation parts (reading) of the interactive exercises.

If you reveal after the assessment that you have a specific learning need, this will not be taken into account in the marking. It will also not be allowed as grounds for appeal in the event of your being unsuccessful.

Travelling to the Assessment Centre

As mentioned above, if you are late arriving you may be prevented from taking part. So make sure you plan your journey in advance, leaving yourself plenty of time for any unforeseen hold-ups. The best way to do this is to undertake a practice journey, preferably at a similar time to when you will travel on the assessment day. Remember, if you do a practice run at the weekend, it may take you much longer on a weekday.

Whether travelling by car or public transport, always ensure you have enough time so that you arrive in a calm manner. If you are unsure whether the Assessment Centre has parking, then check this prior to attending. Having to find alternative parking could add a considerable amount to your total journey time.

Arriving at the Assessment Centre

When you arrive, you will join the other candidates for registration and briefing. You will stay with this group when you do the interactive exercises and interviews. Depending on the size of the room, you may join other groups to complete the written exercises.

Although you will be assigned to a group, you will be required to complete all the exercises and tests on your own.

What to wear

You should be comfortable throughout the assessment, so consider carefully what you intend to wear – you do not want to be too hot or too cold. While you are not judged on your appearance, you have to complete the exercises carrying out a specified job role. Some candidates feel comfortable when completing these exercises wearing clothing appropriate to the role they are required to fulfil. Most candidates, therefore, wear smart clothes.

Avoid carrying bags as these can be a distraction. Likewise, you will be asked to turn off your mobile phone and you will not be allowed to take it with you to any part of the Assessment Centre. So, if possible, leave your mobile phone at home.

GENERAL ASSUMPTION

During the assessment you will be assessed on your appearance.

FACT

Although your clothes should be clean, you are not judged on your appearance unless it is totally inappropriate. This would include, for example, wearing a T-shirt with obscene words on it.

Dress to feel at your best but comfortable. Should you wear, for example, a tie and jacket and then, on the day of your assessment, it becomes very warm, do not be afraid to remove these. It will not affect your assessment in any way.

How to behave

Always treat other candidates and Assessment Centre staff in an appropriate manner, from the moment you arrive to the moment you leave. The ability to treat all people with dignity and respect is a skill all Police Community Support Officers must be able to display. (We will look at this in greater detail in **Chapter 8**.)

GENERAL ASSUMPTION

Your behaviour is only assessed during exercises or the interview.

FACT

While this is true, inappropriate behaviour will be taken into consideration at any time you are at the Assessment Centre, even if you have been told you are on a break. Such behaviour may be taken into account when considering your suitability for an appointment. This may seem unfair, but it is based on the fact that, once appointed as a Police Community Support Officer, you will always be seen as such, so if you behave inappropriately, whether on or off duty, your behaviour will bring your police force adverse comment and publicity. The public, quite rightly, will always expect the behaviour of someone employed by the police service to be of a suitable standard, whether working at that time or not. It would therefore be wrong for a police service to observe unacceptable behaviour and not take this into consideration when making an appointment.

It is difficult to give a list of appropriate and inappropriate behaviour. What you should do is consider the location, audience and circumstances in which any behaviour is being displayed. Police Commmunity Support Officers must be able to adapt to many situations and react appropriately to them all.

As an example, consider swearing. Can you think of a time and place when it would be acceptable for a Police Commmunity Support Officer to swear? Even if you can think of an occasion when swearing may be justified, this does not mean that swearing is acceptable at any time. As a general rule, if in doubt, don't do it!

Briefings during the assessment

All candidates will receive information in the form of verbal briefings at the start of the assessment and then at the beginning of the interview, written and interactive exercises. When giving briefings, the centre's staff read from prepared cards. This may seem strange, but it does ensure you receive the same information as all the other candidates.

At key points in a briefing, you will be given written cards to read to reinforce what you are being told. This will help you understand the key points.

At the end of a briefing, if you are unsure, ask. It is almost certain that others in your group will also be unclear. Asking questions during briefings will not affect your assessment in any way. The invigilators who give the briefings are not involved in the assessment, but they will report on any inappropriate behaviour they observe. The invigilators will do their best to ensure you feel at ease and will make sure you are in the right place for each part of the assessment.

Approaching the interview and exercises

You should attend the Assessment Centre with an open mind, confident that you have the required skills – after all, you will have demonstrated some of these skills in getting through the paper application. Use the skills you have, not a set method for completing the written and interactive exercises. The only formula – such as it is – is to respond appropriately to what you read and to what you are told.

In the interactive exercises, do not assume that the racial origin or sex of the role player is part of the exercise: most exercises are not race or gender specific. Should race or sex be part of the exercise, this will be made clear in the exercise materials.

GENERAL ASSUMPTION

You should adopt a definite system for the assessment exercises. Using a set system or method, or getting in certain buzz words or phrases, is the recipe for success.

FACT

Police work is complicated, if only for the fact that people are involved and no two people are alike. People have different expectations and needs. Equally, no two Police Community Support Officers are the same, and so there is often no right or wrong answer, or just one way of dealing with a policing situation. The same is true of the exercises at the Assessment Centre. Any system will have its weaknesses, and preconceived words or phrases will not help if they are not applicable to the situation or person.

Having said this, what you can do is develop skills and abilities so that you can respond appropriately to what you read or hear. We will explore this further when we consider the interactive and written exercises in detail.

Refreshments

Most assessment centres for Police Community Support Officers will take between two and four hours. This will depend on the number of candidates that are to be assessed during that particular assessment session. However, the facilities at each Assessment Centre vary – some offer refreshments but others are unable to do so, although all should provide drinking water. The Assessment Centre will tell you in advance if you are allowed to bring food with you.

You will know from personal experience that too much food can make you feel tired and lethargic. So avoid overeating. Similarly, even if you feel nervous it is usually better to eat something rather than go for a long period without food. This is particularly important if you made an early start and so did without breakfast.

Comfort breaks

Comfort breaks will be offered throughout the assessment. It is important you take advantage of these because, if you need to take a break at any time during an exercise or the interview, you will not be allowed any extra time to complete these on your return.

Speaking to other candidates

There are no tasks that require you to consult with the other candidates. So formal exam conditions apply to all the exercises and the interview. Between exercises and the interview, however, you are allowed to speak to the other candidates, but avoid being drawn into conversations regarding what has taken place or what happens next. The Assessment Centre is about your completing the exercises and interview to the best of your own abilities.

Listening to what others have done will, at best, confirm that what you did was the same as others or, at worst, cause you to have doubts. If you discuss future exercises, this may cause you to be indecisive or to do something you may not otherwise have done. It is very unlikely this would be to your advantage. Therefore, restrict any conversations you have with the other candidates to small talk. Should you hear discussions about the exercises and tests, try to avoid listening and certainly do not join in.

It is worth repeating that, as well as avoiding entering into conversations at the Assessment Centre, you should be very careful about obtaining information from websites or others who have previously completed the assessment, even if they have been successful.

If you have preconceived ideas about the exercises, it is likely you will have made up your mind as to the actions and decisions you will take. This may stop you asking appropriate questions or listening to what you are being told, and this will consequently impact negatively on your performance.

Fitness and substance abuse testing

All police forces will require candidates to undergo some form of medical and fitness scrutiny and some forces may require candidates to be tested for substance abuse. These may, or may not be carried out on the same day as the Assessment Centre. Check with the service to which you have applied as to what additional tests will be carried out and when.

> ## TOP TIPS
>
> - Make sure you take with you the required identification evidence.
>
> - Make sure you have received and have read the latest information documents.
>
> - Discuss any specific needs you may have prior to attending for your assessment.
>
> - Know the route (and any alternative routes) to the Assessment Centre.
>
> - Allow plenty of time for travelling.
>
> - Dress appropriately but make sure you are comfortable.
>
> - At all times treat everyone with dignity and respect.
>
> - Have sufficient refreshment prior to assessment.
>
> - Take advantage of comfort breaks.
>
> - Avoid discussions with your fellow candidates.
>
> - Be wary of information you are given by candidates who have attended previously.
>
> - Be wary of information contained in unofficial websites.
>
> - Check on the content and timing of any additional tests.

INDIVIDUAL LEARNING POINTS

Chapter 5
Interactive Exercises

Introduction

The interactive exercises involve you role playing someone who has a specific job in an organisation. You will be provided with information concerning a situation or an incident that has occurred in this organisation, and you will have to deal with someone who is involved in this situation or incident in some way, role playing the person whose job you have been given.

Each interactive exercise is made up of two five-minute parts. There is a 90-second gap between each part. In the first part, you prepare for the role play on your own. In the second, you meet the person who is role acting the other part in the situation or incident, and it is in this part that you must deal with his or her issue or concern. There are two interactive exercises in total, each lasting $11\frac{1}{2}$ minutes. The number of exercises may be increased or reduced, but the principles behind them will remain the same.

Your role

Before you attend the Assessment Centre you will be sent an outline of the job you will role play, along with any background information you may require. This information will contain any policies that may be of help to you during the exercises. You should read and try to understand these, but you do not need to learn them off by heart. If you want to refer to these during the exercises, they will be available for you to consult. It is, however, important that you have a good grasp of these before you attend.

In addition to receiving the job description and the background material, you will also receive a brief explanation of the Assessment Centre. This will contain the names of the two interactive exercises you will be required to undertake. After the name of each exercise will be a brief description of that exercise (for example, 'Allen wishes to discuss an incident he witnessed at the hospital').

Part one of an interactive exercise

In this part of the exercise you are given written information about the issue or incident and about the person you will meet (an example of this material is provided later in this chapter). Always read this information slowly and deliberately so that you are clear as to what it is you are being asked to do.

You will be provided with paper and pens so that you can make notes. While you are not allowed to take the original information with you to part two of the exercise, you can take your notes. These are not assessed.

Use your notes to:

- write down any key points;

- write down any points that require clarification;

- identify any appropriate questions;

- identify any information that should be given by you to the role actor; and

- identify potential options for dealing with the situation.

Simply list these points briefly so that you can use them as reminders. Do not make too many notes. If you do, you will not be able to pick out the key points when you meet the role actor. Try to keep your notes to no more than one side of A4. Keep them clear, simple and easy to read.

Part two of an interactive exercise

You will enter a room where you will meet the person you are required to deal with. Also in this room, seated, will be an assessor. If a third person is present, he or she is there to monitor the exercise, not you. This person will also be seated, close to the assessor. The person you will speak to will be very evident as he or she will be wearing a name badge appropriate to the exercise. This person will usually speak to you when you enter the room.

On a chair near to the role actor will be a copy of the information you read in part one. It will be the same: you do not need to check to see if it contains changed or additional information. Should you need to refer to this information, do so.

When dealing with the role actor, do not be afraid to use your notes to make sure you raise all the issues and questions you need to raise. Do not be afraid to take the time to do this: you are not required to fill silences, however tempting this may be, and you are not penalised for periods of silence. If appropriate, use the chair provided to sit on. One will also have been provided for the role actor. It is usually appropriate to remain seated throughout the five minutes.

You are not allowed to write during part two of the exercise. Should you do so, you will be reminded at the end of the five minutes not to do so. No further action will be taken.

GENERAL ASSUMPTION

The exercises are unfair because you would not normally deal with such issues within a five-minute period.

> **FACT**
>
> You are only required to do what is possible within the five minutes. You can score very well even if you do not reach a conclusion.

The checklists the assessors use to monitor your performance were devised after watching numerous mock candidates complete the exercises within the same time frame. Like you, these mock candidates will have been provided with only five minutes' preparation time and five minutes' activity time.

These mock candidates are selected from a variety of situations that reflect potential Police Community Support Officers, so they should reflect the potential actions and behaviours of would-be candidates. What the majority of these mock candidates were able to achieve within the five minutes is reflected in the assessors' marking guides.

Moving from one exercise to the next

You will be fully briefed before beginning the interactive exercises. All candidates are required to complete two exercises in total. This represents four periods of five minutes, with 90 seconds between each. Usually candidates complete the exercises in syndicates of four, although individual candidates complete each individual exercise alone. The size of the syndicate can vary, for example increased to six, whereby each candidate would complete one exercise, have a break of eleven and half minutes and then complete the next exercise. Do not be concerned by this as you will be fully briefed on your assessment day.

A buzzer or whistle signals the end of each five minutes or 90 seconds. Do not worry if you do not hear the signal: an assessor will ensure you move at the appropriate time and to the right place. Each of the two exercises is stand-alone. You do not, therefore, need to take any information from one exercise to the next.

During the briefing you will be told at which exercise to start. Usually the preparation areas will be numbered one and three and where you meet and deal with the role actor will be numbered two and four. You will always start at a preparation area but it could be room one or three.

Candidates will usually be numbered one, two, three or four and candidates one and three will be taken to stand outside their respective preparation areas. Therefore candidate number one will stand outside the preparation area or room marked number one and candidate three will stand at the preparation area or room marked number three. They will subsequently move around each of the marked rooms in numerical order. Candidate one will move through two, three and four, and candidate three, will first move to four followed by one and two.

Candidates who have even numbers are taken on to the assessment floor five minutes after the odd-numbered candidates. They are told to begin at the number one up from their candidate number. For example, a candidate has been allocated the number two.

When he or she is taken on to the assessment floor, he or she will begin at number three. Number four however, will start at number one. The reason for this is that candidates can only commence at a preparation part of an exercise.

The interactive exercise assessment floor will be laid out similar to the diagram below. You move round the exercises as indicated by the arrows.

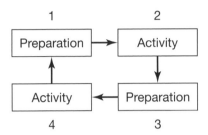

Example exercise

Before continuing, read the information pack in **Appendix C**. You should understand the role you are required to fulfil and the policies relevant to your role and the organisation.

Now read the sample exercise called 'Collins'. Try to keep this reading to five minutes to reflect Assessment Centre conditions. Make any notes you think appropriate in the space labelled 'Candidate notes'. Keep these short. Remember, if this was an exercise at an Assessment Centre, the printed information would be available to you in both parts of the exercise, so you do not have to record too much detail. Make notes to jog your memory about those things you would want to say or ask the role actor, and about your potential solutions.

Interactive Exercises

Collins

Candidate information

In this exercise there are three pages of pre-information:

1 A general report from Paul Reeve, a First Contact Officer.
2 An incident report from Ranjit Batra, a Mobile First Contact Support Officer.
3 A copy of the Central Trust's Lost Person Policy.

Following the preparation period, you will meet Binney Collins.

Central Hospital Trust

General Report

From: Paul Reeve – First Contact Officer
To: Candidate – Mobile First Contact Support Officer
Date: Yesterday 2.00 pm
Subject: Binney Collins

Yesterday at 2pm Binney Collins attended the hospital with her 4-year-old daughter Charlotte. She was visiting an elderly relative on Dryden Ward. While speaking to him and dealing with his needs Charlotte wandered away from the bed and out of the ward.

Mobile First Contact Support Officer Ranjit Batra attended and dealt with this. His report of the incident is attached. On returning home Collins contacted the hospital by phone complaining of the lack of action by the hospital.

I have arranged for Collins to visit the hospital to discuss her concerns and would normally deal with this myself but unfortunately have a prior engagement, could you therefore see her on my behalf and deal with her as you think appropriately.

Paul Reeve

Paul Reeve

First Contact Officer

Central Hospital Trust

Incident report

From: Ranjit Batra, Mobile First Contact Support Officer
To: Paul Reeve – First Contact Officer
Date: Yesterday 2.00 pm
Subject: Binney Collins, 41 Paris Walk, Central Town, Telephone 587806

Yesterday at 2pm I attended Dryden Ward to see a Binney Collins regarding her missing child Charlotte aged 4 years.

As per the policy I contacted the Police for them to attend to deal. I waited with Collins but within 20 minutes another visitor had found Charlotte and returned her to her mother.

On the child being found I cancelled the Police before they could attend.

No other action was taken.

R. Batra

Ranjit Batra

Mobile First Contact Support Officer

Central Hospital Trust

Lost Person Policy

Patients can be lost for a variety of reasons and visitors to the hospital can often be emotional for a variety of reasons and should they have care of children it is easy for them to allow the children to walk away.

Experience has shown that once adults or children become lost they can rapidly reach all parts of the hospital buildings or grounds, or even leave the premises totally.

Should an adult or child be reported missing either by a member of staff or a member of the public then a Mobile First Contact Support Officer should attend immediately and take the following actions: -

- Notify the Police
- Identify to the Police a fixed point of contact for them to attend at the hospital to take control
- Commence a written log of any actions taken
- Get a description of the missing adult or child
- Circulate the information to First Contact Officers for onward distribution to their respective Mobile First Contact Support Officers
- If a member of the public reported the missing person ensure that someone remains with them until the police are in attendance
- Conduct an immediate search of the area from where the adult or child was last seen
- Be present when the Police attend and provide any help and assistance as requested by the Police

This should not be considered an exhaustive list and any other actions in addition to the above, should be taken if considered appropriate at the time.

Candidate's notes

Having completed your preparation for the exercise 'Collins' look at your notes and the questions you have prepared. Have you considered asking Binney Collins the following?

- Collins' contact details?
- What happened?
- What was said?
- Confirmed Batra's account as accurate with Collins?

Also consider the things you would want to tell Collins, such as:

- Identify you are there to deal with the incident on behalf of Reeve
- Outline the lost person policy
- Inform Collins of Batra's actions, which were correct
- Identify that the missing child was found quickly.

Lastly have you considered the personal factors for Collins and potential solutions?

- Apologise for the policy not being followed
- Ask if Charlotte has recovered from being lost
- Ask Collins if they have recovered from their child being lost
- Ask how Collins would like this to be resolved
- Suggest a course of action
- Explain how feedback will be given to Collins following this meeting.

This may appear a lot to consider in five minutes preparation but candidates readily process key questions and issues. Remember to only make bullet points. Candidates do not usually have time to write their notes in full. As an alternative rather than writing the questions separately you could list general areas such as:

- Ask what happened
- Outline what should have happened
- Outline what went according to policy
- Outline what didn't go according to policy
- Check on the welfare of those involved
- Seek a resolution and ask how feedback should be provided.

Similarly, you could record key words for the issues you wish to raise and for your suggested solutions.

The 90-second interval

During this time you will move from the preparation area to go to stand outside the activity room where you will meet the role actor. This will literally take seconds. Use the remaining time to consider a structure for dealing with the role actor, but remember that you are not allowed to write during the 90 seconds.

A structured format for dealing with this and similar exercises would be as follows:

- *Collect information from the role actor*: first, ask the role actor appropriate questions to obtain all the information you require to understand fully what happened and to establish who else was present.

- *Give the role actor information*: give the role actor any information he or she appears not to have and outline any appropriate policies or issues.

- *Discuss potential solutions*: in consultation with the role actor, explore potential solutions to the situation. If appropriate, consider short, medium and long-term solutions.

- *State your proposed actions*: outline your intended course of action. In addition, identify whom you intend to give feedback to and how this will take place. Where possible, gain agreement from the role actor with regards to your proposed course of action. Do not be put off if the role actor does not give his or her definite approval – it would be unusual for him or her to do so.

What happens during the second part of the exercise?

After 90 seconds, on hearing the signal, enter the room and deal with the role actor as you think appropriate. You do not need to knock before entering, and you will see the role actor you are required to deal with. (As mentioned previously, he or she will have a badge that clearly identifies him or her.)

The role actor will usually have an opening line to deliver to you. After he or she has delivered this, talk to him or her as you would to anyone else during a normal conversation. Try to control any nerves you may have and listen to what the role actor is saying. Resist the temptation to start talking immediately as this will stop the role actor from delivering his or her first line. Do not be afraid to use your notes or the provided printed exercise information.

Should you dry up during the five minutes, the role actor will look away to the floor. If this happens, the assessor will tell you that you can start talking again if you wish at any time during the five minutes. You are not penalised for pauses, however long. When you start again, no explanation or apology is required: just continue as if there had been no break. The role actor will immediately re-engage with you.

The signal will then be given that indicates the end of the exercise. If you continue after this signal, the assessor will simply ask you to leave the room. Do not, therefore, try to continue, as nothing you say after the five minutes will be scored and you are reducing the time you have available to move to the next preparation area or room.

How behaviours are scored

The assessor looks at his or her checklist to see if the questions or statements you make or ask are listed there. If they are, the relevant question or statement is ticked as having been achieved. On the assessor's checklist your questions and statements are referred to as 'behaviours'.

There are usually between 12 and 18 behaviours on an exercise checklist. Groups of similar behaviours are listed together under the appropriate competency area. If you look at the suggested questions and statements for the sample exercise 'Collins', the first set would be recorded under the heading 'Effective Communication', the second under 'Resilience' and the third under 'Community and Customer Focus'.

If you look at the National Core Competencies listed in **Appendix A**, you will see how the groups of behaviours relate to those areas. As an example, consider the first set of questions. If you look at the positive indicators under the competency area 'Effective Communication', you will see how asking those questions would relate to the following positive indicators:

- Asks questions to clarify issues

- Makes sure information is factual, accurate and provided at the right time

- Makes sure communication has a clear purpose

In addition to scoring the behaviours, the assessors have to decide how well each individual behaviour was achieved. The assessors are given clear guidelines about this during their training, and they are also given descriptors (called 'scalars') within the bounds of which their decisions must be taken.

Consider again the questions from the Collins example. The scalar used for these questions would be something like 'thorough to vague'. For example you wish to confirm Collins' contact details. You can achieve this in a numbers of ways by asking Collins, the role actor, the following questions:

- Please give me your full name, address and telephone number, and a mobile number if you have one.

- Please give me your contact details.

- If I need to could I contact you at Paris Walk?

- Are your details as per the Mobile First Contact Support Officer's report? (This without showing Batra's report to them to see the details)

All these examples are ways of finding out the contact details for Collins, but the first is thorough, the second less so and the final two are vague. As a general rule, if you say exactly what is on the checklist, you will be awarded a mid-point scalar score.

GENERAL ASSUMPTION

You do better if you score lots of behaviours on the assessor's checklist.

FACT

What you do (behaviours) and how you do them (scalars) are of equal importance. Therefore, you can perform a few of the identified behaviours well, yet still score the same (or better) than someone who does lots of behaviours badly. The reason for this is simple: in dealing with the public it is very often not what you do that is important, but how you actually do it. Many complaints against the police are not based on what the employee actually did but the way they did it.

The area Respect for Race and Diversity and a candidate's oral communication skills are also assessed in the interactive exercises, but usually without descriptive behaviours.

How Respect for Race and Diversity is scored

Respect for Race and Diversity is taken into consideration for everything you do during the five minutes you interact with the role actor. There are, however, usually no stated behaviours for the assessor to monitor. All your statements and questions can be considered, and the assessors will have been provided with instructions to guide their observations. This normally takes the form of two short, descriptive sentences. Using the example 'Collins', these would typically be as follows:

- Deals with the role actor in a sensitive way.

- Uses appropriate language and terms with regards to all the involved parties and issues.

In addition to these sentences, scalars are also used. Again using 'Collins' as an example:

- Sentence 1 would be 'Sensitive' to 'Insensitive'.

- Sentence 2 would be 'Appropriate' to 'Inappropriate'.

If your actions do not fall within the prescribed parameters for assessment, but the behaviour you display is inappropriate, this will still be recorded and could result in your being awarded a grade D (this is explained in more detail in **Chapter 8**).

How your oral communication skills are scored

The assessors are asked to consider two things about the way you speak:

- Can they hear what you say?

- Can they understand what you are saying?

The assessors will do this by taking into account factors similar to those listed below:

- Can the candidate be heard?

- Can the candidate be understood?

- Is the language used inappropriate or jargon?

- Is there structure to it?

- Is it appropriate for the audience?

- Are the responses appropriate to the other person?

- Does the candidate interrupt and over-talk?

As in the competency area Respect for Race and Diversity, this is described in two sentences:

- Can be heard and is structured and logical.

- Uses appropriate language.

Again, there would be two scalars:

- Sentence 1 would be 'Clear' to 'Unclear'.

- Sentence 2 would be 'Appropriate' to 'Inappropriate'.

These factors will be taken into consideration for everything you say during the five minutes. You should not worry too much about structure, even if you are not able to follow the structure you wanted to – just make sure you respond appropriately to the role actor. You will not be penalised for this.

This part of the assessment is simply to ensure that you can be understood and that you can link questions and answers logically together. Most candidates have no difficulty in achieving the required standard in this area.

Example assessor's checklist

Below is an example of an assessor's checklist using the 'Collins' exercise. On the left are the behaviours the assessors are looking for you to demonstrate. In the middle are the scalar descriptors for scoring a behaviour. On the right are the grade options (A–D).

'Collins' exercise checklist

Behaviours	Scalar	Grade
Effective Communication		A, B, C, D
1.1 Ask/confirm Collins contact details	Thorough to vague	
1.2 Ask what happened	Thorough to vague	
1.3 Ask what was said	Thorough to vague	
1.4 Confirm Batra's account as accurate with Collins	Thorough to vague	

Behaviours	Scalar	Grade
Resilience		A, B, C, D
2.1 Identify that they are there to deal with the incident on behalf of Reeve	Clear to unclear	
2.2 Outline the lost person policy	Clear to unclear	
2.3 Inform Collins of Batra's actions which were correct	Clear to unclear	
2.4 Identify that the missing child was found quickly	Clear to unclear	
Community and Customer focus		A, B, C, D
3.1 Ask Collins if they are over their child being lost	Confident to unsure	
3.2 Ask if Charlotte has got over being lost	Confident to unsure	
3.3 Apologise for the policy not being followed	Confident to unsure	
3.4 Ask how Collins wishes for this to be resolved	Confident to unsure	
3.5 Suggest a course of action	Confident to unsure	
3.6 Agree how they will give feedback to Collins following this meeting	Confident to unsure	
Respect for Race and Diversity		A, B, C, D
4.1 Deals with the role actor in a sensitive way	Sensitive to Insensitive	
4.2 Uses appropriate language and terms in dealing with all involved parties and issues	Appropriate to Inappropriate	
Oral communication skills		A, B, C, D
5.1 Can be heard and is structured and logical	Clear to unlcear	
5.2 Uses appropriate language	Appropriate to Inappropriate	

How a competency area is scored

At the end of the five minutes the assessor considers each competency area in turn, noting how many behaviours the candidate has scored and how well these were performed. Scalars are assessed on a scale of 1–5 (1 being the highest score). From these two scores, the candidate is awarded a grade for that competency area, from A to D (A being the highest).

An example for Effective Communication is as follows. A candidate demonstrates only one behaviour by saying 'Was something said to you?'. This behaviour would be marked as scored at 1.3 on the checklist. The assessor would then decide how thoroughly or vaguely the question was asked. It would be scored 1 if it was considered totally thorough and 5 if vague. In this case, it would probably be given a score of 5: the candidate did not ask *what* was said but whether something had been said. As a general rule, it is always best to ask open questions – questions that, usually, cannot be answered with just one word.

Think of how a parent might ask his or her child about the child's day at school. The parent could ask: 'Did you have a good day at school?' This is a closed question – he or she would probably receive a one-word answer (yes or no). If the parent asked an open question ('What did you do at school today?'), this should receive a more detailed answer.

The assessor looks at these two indicators (the behaviours and the scalar) and then awards a grade – in this case a D. This is because the candidate showed only one of the required behaviours in that competency area, and he or she did not do this very well.

A further example using Resilience would be as follows. The candidate scores 2.4 by saying 'Charlotte was found in a very short period of time'. This would attract a scalar of 3 because the candidate did very similar to what was on the checklist – no better or worse than the mid-point on the scalar. The candidate could then go on to score 2.2 by reading the lost person policy to the role actor. Because the candidate can do no more in terms of displaying this behaviour, he or she would most likely attract a scalar of 1. These two scores produce an average scalar for that competency area of 2. The final grade is calculated by combining the overall scalar with the number of behaviours scored. In this example it would result in a B grade being awarded.

With regards to Respect for Race and Diversity and oral communication skills, the assessor will consider what the candidate said during the five minutes. He or she will use the sentence descriptors and the scalars to award a grade for each of these.

As can be seen from these examples, you do not have to say exactly what is on the checklist in order to score. In addition, you can ask questions or make statements at any time during the five minutes, and this will not affect the grade you will achieve. For example, early in the five minutes a candidate scores a 1.1 and a 1.2. Towards the end of the five minutes, the candidate scores the behaviour 1.4. The fact that the candidate did not do these behaviours as a group will not affect how the assessor considers the scalar together for each behaviour and the candidate's overall grade.

The Role Actors

In addition to training in assessment and role acting, the role actors are trained in the exercises they will perform. They aim to give the same performance for each candidate: they will not react in any way to the candidate's actions and attitudes, other than to give the prescribed responses to the statements made or the questions asked. They respond in the manner they have been asked to portray.

The role actors are given background information regarding the roles they will play, plus set responses to the candidates' questions and statements. These set responses are derived from observing mock candidates during the design and development of that particular exercise. A role actor will usually have between 12 and 20 lines. They must learn these off by heart so that each candidate receives the same information. In addition, the role actors must understand the potential questions and statements from candidates so that they can deliver the prescribed lines at the correct time.

Below is an example of a role actor's instructions for the 'Collins' exercise. Obviously you will not see these instructions, but they will show you what type of information the role actor receives and should give you the confidence that all candidates receive the same experiences and opportunities.

Role Actor's Instructions

Background information

Your name is Binney Collins and you visited Dryden Ward to visit an elderly relative who has been in hospital for approximately two weeks following a broken hip but who is making a good recovery. Being a single parent you had no alternative but to take your 4 year old daughter, Charlotte, with you. Your details are as recorded on Batra's report. You have no mobile phone and can be contacted at home any evening after 6pm.

While dealing with your relative, although you only turned your back for a minute, Charlotte walked off and you could not readily locate her.

The Ward Sister got a Mobile First Contact Support Officer to attend and help you, and although he attended quickly, all he did was sit with you and call the police. Despite you being frantic with worry and wanting to go and look he insisted you remain with him for the police to arrive.

Having reflected on the incident when you arrived home you telephoned the Hospital to complain.

While you were very angry at the hospital's lack of action you are now very calm. You just want to make sure this does not happen again and will accept any suggestions made to resolve it.

Prompts and scripted lines

- When the candidate enters the room say, 'My name is Binney Collins I want to complain, your hospital did nothing to help me find my daughter'

- If the candidate asks what happened say, 'Your Mobile First Contact Support Officer just made me wait with him 'til the police came'

- If the candidate asks what Batra said, say, 'He just kept saying the police are the professionals, just wait for them to come and they would deal with it'

- If the candidate shows/outline Batra's report and asks if it is correct say, 'That's right it's terrible, I want something done'

- If the candidate asks if your contact details are correct, whether they show you Batra's report or not say, 'They are as I gave them on the phone'

- If the candidate outlines the lost person's policy say, 'That's all well and good, but that didn't happen'

- If the candidate explains which parts of the policy were followed say, 'But most of the policy wasn't followed'

- If the candidate apologises for the lack of action say, 'Thank-you for that but it won't stop it happening again'

- If the candidate asks if you are over the distress of losing your daughter say, 'I'm fine now thank-you'

- If the candidate asks if Charlotte is still upset at getting lost say, 'She never had a problem, I don't even think she knew she was lost'

- If the candidate asks how you would like it resolved say, 'I'm not really sure, I'll be guided by you'

- If the candidate suggests resolutions say, 'I'm happy to go with whatever you think, provided the same thing doesn't happen to anyone else'.

You do not have to give the questions or statements as per the role actor's prompts in order to get the response, but they do have to have the same meaning. Should you ask questions or make statements that do not have a scripted line, the role actors will keep their answers as short as possible. However, their responses will be within the confines of the background information.

It is very important that you listen to what the role actor is saying and respond to this. While you will have a plan for dealing with the situation and will have considered what questions and statements you want to ask or make, you have to be flexible and must respond appropriately to the role actor.

What happens if you finish before the end of the five minutes?

You should not be concerned if you finish before the signal for the end of the exercise. As mentioned previously, should this happen, the role actor will simply look at the floor. You are not allowed to leave the room and, should you wish to start again at any time, simply recommence the conversation. You are not penalised for silences and nor should you try to engage the role actor or assessor in small talk as neither will respond. Even if you indicate that you have finished, the assessor will tell you that you can carry on at any time within the five minutes, should you wish to do so.

As a general rule, if you finish before the end, go back to the start and recap on what you and the role actor have said and agreed. This will assist your memory and can very often spur you on to ask further questions or to seek clarification (remember, you cannot score during a silence). Remember, many candidates finish before the end of the five minutes but still score very well.

What not to have with you

Bleepers and mobile phones

During the briefing for the interactive exercises, you will be told not to carry any items that give off sounds. This is to prevent candidates mistaking the sound these make for the sound that indicates the start or finish of the exercises. Some candidates think they can use bleepers or mobile phones as an alarm to signal they are nearing the end of the five minutes. This is not, however, allowed, and such devices will be taken from you if you try to use them in this way. While you will not be penalised for this, it may affect your concentration if you are told to turn off your bleeper or mobile phone.

Written information

In addition to bleepers and mobile phones, you are not allowed to take the information you were sent prior to attending the Assessment Centre or any notes you made before attending into the exercises and tests. Such information could give you an unfair advantage over the other candidates and, should you consult this information during your assessment, it is likely this would cause you to fail, no matter how well you perform in the assessment itself.

TOP TIPS

- Read the information you are provided within the preparation phase slowly and carefully.
- Make notes in list form that will act as memory joggers when you meet the role actor in part two of the exercise.
- Take your notes from the preparation phase with you and use them.
- Use the information you are given in the activity room to check the details, if necessary.
- Do not make assumptions based on the role actor's racial origin or sex.
- Listen to the role actor and respond to what he or she says.
- Do not write during the 90-second interval or when you meet the role actor.
- Give the role actor time to say his or her opening line when you enter the room.
- Use open rather than closed questions.
- If you finish before the end of the five minutes, recap on what you have asked the role actor, his or her responses and the agreed actions.

INDIVIDUAL LEARNING POINTS

_____

_____

_____

_____

_____

_____

_____

_____

_____

_____

Chapter 6
Written Exercises

Introduction

A key part of a Police Community Support Officer's role is to record information and, subsequently, to write up this information in such documents as statements of evidence. These documents must be both legible and understandable. The written tests assess your basic writing skills rather than your knowledge of the finer points of English grammar. The assessors are looking for candidates who can produce written information that is legible, accurate and easy to understand. Reread the competency area Effective Communication and this will indicate the matters that will be considered when assessing candidates' written abilities.

GENERAL ASSUMPTION

In the written exercises the assessors are looking to assess candidates' written ability against detailed punctuation checklists.

FACT

Assessors are not looking to penalise candidates for the misuse of speech marks, question marks etc. They are looking to see sentences that can be understood and words spelt correctly.

The number of written exercises

There are two written exercises. In both you must read and understand some information and then provide a written response to this information, as instructed in the exercise.

Briefing

Before the exercises, you will be fully briefed as to what is expected of you. You will be told where you should record your candidate number, the time limit for each exercise and how the exercises are conducted. You will also be told what to do if you make a mistake. As with the other briefings, to make sure you understand them fully, you will be asked to read certain instructions while the invigilator reads them out aloud.

Outline of a written exercise

The written exercises are very similar to the interactive exercises, the main difference being that, in the written exercises, you write your response down rather than speak it. Each written exercise has a time limit of 20 minutes, which includes time for you to read the exercise.

At the start of each exercise you will be provided with the exercise itself, pens and a form on which to write your response. Extra sheets are available if you run out of space on the form, and you will be provided with paper on which you can make rough notes.

How to approach the written exercises

Read through the exercise and think carefully about the task you have been set. Do not rush this: a few extra minutes spent considering the exercise and task will save you time later.

You write your response using the same job role you used for the interactive exercises. As before, if you need a policy from the information pack, this will be provided. Again, it is important you read and understand the information sent to you prior to attending for assessment. This should make reading the policies at the Assessment Centre a memory jog rather than having to understand them from scratch.

Be very clear as to what you must provide in your response. Before you write your final answer, make a list of all those things you want to mention. This will help you to focus on the key points you must cover.

TASK 1

Read the example written exercise on pages 58–60, but do not complete the blank general report form until you have done Task 2 and read Task 3.

Written Exercises

'Traffic Flow'

Candidate information

In this exercise there are two pages of pre-information:

1 A general report from Paul Reeve, the First Contact Officer.
2 A copy of the Mobile First Contact Support Officer's job description.

You are required to provide a written response.

Central Hospital Trust

General Report

From:	Paul Reeve – First Contact Officer
To:	Candidate – Mobile First Contact Support Officer
Date:	Two days ago
Subject:	Traffic Flow

The peak times for patients and visitors arriving at the hospital by car is between 9.30am – 10.30am and 2pm – 3pm.

The car park at the centre of the hospital holds 250 cars and this quickly becomes full during these times causing a line of cars to form down the road that leads to its entrance. This line builds up along this road and can block a roundabout at one of the entrance points to the hospital. This can affect emergency vehicles and patient appointments.

The other three remaining car parks located at the edges of the hospital usually do not become full.

Please write a report to me outlining the issues and potential actions you and other mobile first contact support officers should take to assist in resolving this.

Paul Reeve

Paul Reeve

First Contact Officer

Central Hospital Trust

Mobile First Contact Support Officer's Job Description

Mobile First Contact Support Officers work at fixed points within the hospital and also patrol the hospital's buildings and grounds. Both of these duties are under the guidance and direction of their appointed First Contact Officer.

Times at fixed points, which will usually be at entrances to wards and departments, will be to cover for absences of First Contact Officers. This should be kept to a minimum.

Patrol by Mobile First Contact Support Officers can be self directed or targeted to observe and deal with issues as identified by their First Contact Officer.

The duty times will be agreed to ensure cover between 8.00 am and 10.00 pm.

Their main responsibilities under the direction of their First Contact Officer will be as follows:

- To act as a point of contact for all non medical issues for patients and visitors

- To receive, enquire into and resolve any concerns, non medical, from staff, patients or visitors

- To complete written reports on all matters reported to them

- To ensure the Patient Confidentiality Policy is adhered to and explained fully to patients and visitors when required. They will also be available to give staff advice on this issue

- To enforce, as required, the no smoking policy with staff, patients and visitors

- To give advice to staff, patients and visitors on the Equality Policy

- To assist First Contact Officer's in ensuring all Trust policies and procedures are complied with

- To work with the parking and shop managers regarding security and provision of services

- To provide assistance, as required, following the activation of fire or security alarms

- To deal, in the first instance, with non-hospital related issues such as lost children or drunk and abusive patients or visitors

- To ensure the free flow of traffic around the roads within the hospital complex.

Central Hospital Trust

General report

From: Candidate – Mobile First Contact Support Officer
To: Paul Reeve – First Contact Officer
Date: Today's date
Subject: Proposal for 'Traffic Flow'

_____

_____

_____

_____

_____

_____

_____

_____

_____

_____

_____

_____

_____

_____

_____

_____

_____

_____

_____

_____

_____

_____

TASK 2

When you are clear about what you have been asked to do, write in list form what you think should be included in your written response. Make sure you outline the issues and the potential actions. As with the notes you make for the interactive exercises, you are the only person who will read these, so they do not have to be written in full. Single words will often be enough. Now compare your list with the one below.

Example issues:

- Traffic backing up on the roundabout could stop or delay emergency vehicles getting through

- The delays could cause patients to be late for appointments

- Both the above could have serious consequences for patients and also affect the efficiency of the hospital

- The lack of use of other car parks

Example actions:

- Ensure Mobile First Contact Officers patrol near to the central car park and adjoining roads to prevent traffic building up

- Ensure Mobile First Contact Support Officers patrol the required areas between 9.30am – 10.30am and 2pm – 3pm

- Mobile First Contact Support Officers to move on stationary cars waiting on roads

- Mobile First Contact Support Officers to direct vehicles stationary on a road to the other car parks

- Consider signs to direct vehicles to other car parks

- The access road to the central car park to be closed when the car park is full and only emergency vehicles to be allowed to use it

---

TASK 3

Using your list to guide you, write your full written response on the form provided. Do this within the 20 minutes you will be allocated when you do these exercises at the Assessment Centre.

Your written response should be in complete sentences and paragraphs. You can, however, use lists within this structure, if appropriate. Apart from this, there is no set way you should present your answers.

If you make a mistake or want any part of your response to be ignored, simply put a diagonal line through it. You should also put a diagonal line through your planning list, even if this is on a separate sheet. Anything you write at the Assessment Centre will be collected and anything not crossed through will be marked.

How the written exercises are assessed

The marking scheme is very similar to that for the interactive exercises. The assessor will look at your response to see whether you have included the identified behaviours on his or her checklist, and he or she will also consider how well you have tackled these.

For example, identifying that an action would be for Mobile First Contact Support Officers to patrol the central car park and adjoining roads would be listed as a behaviour. If a candidate stated it may help if someone could patrol in the area, this would score but not very well. Stating that Mobile First Contact Support Officers should patrol the central car park and appropriate identified access roads to prevent a build up of traffic, on the other hand, would be a very strong way of scoring.

In addition to the behaviours, your written English will be assessed considering the following types of questions:

- Can it be read?

- Is it structured in sentence and paragraph form?

- Are words spelt incorrectly?

- Are the correct words used?

- Are there full stops at the end of sentences, followed by capitals?

- Are words missed out of sentences?

Before you continue, assess your report for written English using the above as a marking guide. If you are uncertain about how to do this, ask someone else to look at it for you.

At the Assessment Centre, only use words you know the meaning of. For example: 'Their are four outlets that have made calls for assistance.' You are unsure whether 'their' should be 'there'. If this is the case, think of an alternative way of saying the same thing (for example, 'four outlets have made calls for assistance'). Also make sure that you only use words you can spell correctly.

Use easy-to-understand sentences, and make sure your writing is legible. If you need to develop your skills in this area, write short accounts of everyday happenings (such as a day at work) and ask someone who has the appropriate skills to read them. Ask this person to use the list above as a marking guide.

To work out a candidate's grade for his or her standard of written English, the assessor adds up the number of mistakes the candidate has made in his or her response. This number is compared with a grid that shows which grade is awarded for that number of mistakes. As in the other exercises, the grade range is A–D.

Time

As mentioned above, you have 20 minutes to complete each written exercise. As well as there being a clock in the room, you will be told when there are five minutes remaining, then one minute remaining.

Don't worry if you do not finish: don't sacrifice quality for speed. If your response cannot be read, it cannot be scored. Illegible answers will be counted as mistakes, and this will affect your grade. If you do finish before the end, use this time to check your work thoroughly.

GENERAL ASSUMPTION

The more you write in the 20 minutes, the better your score.

FACT

Quantity is not a key factor in the scoring. While you want to achieve as many of the behaviours on the assessment checklist as possible, the quality of your writing is also important. You can score a lot of things on the checklist badly or a few things well and still achieve a similar overall grade. The key to success is reducing errors to the minimum or eradicating them completely.

Practise beforehand so that you know roughly how much writing you can produce within a 20-minute period. This practice will also ensure that you include all the key elements in your response.

TOP TIPS

- Look at the competency area "Effective Communication" noting the required written standards.
- Identify clearly what is required in the written response to each exercise.
- Before you begin your response, make a list to structure the key elements of your answer.
- Write legibly.
- Only use words you can spell.
- Only use words you know the meaning of.
- Write simple sentences.
- Use full stops at the end of sentences and capital letters at the beginning of sentences.
- Use paragraphs to structure your answer.
- Cross out any writing you do not want marked.
- Use the 20 minutes to the full.

INDIVIDUAL LEARNING POINTS

_____

_____

_____

_____

_____

_____

_____

_____

_____

Chapter 7
Interviews

Introduction

Assessment Centre interviews have been designed very carefully and they are not like typical job interviews. They have been designed so that every candidate is given the same information and questions and, therefore, the same opportunity to demonstrate his or her skills and abilities.

Although water should be available during the interview, many of the pleasantries that are used to start a typical job interview will not be present. Be ready for this, and do not let it put you off.

The questions

You will be asked to talk about the ways you have used your abilities in the past – past behaviour is a good indicator of future performance. For example, a typical question would be: 'Please tell me about an occasion when you worked as part of a team to complete a goal or task.'

Another type of question is to give you a set of circumstances and to ask you what you would do in that situation. For example: 'You are working with someone who you know is lying about his or her part in an incident in order to absolve him or herself of any responsibility, when actually he or she is to blame. What would you do?'

Whatever form of question is used, the issues to consider when answering them are the same, and it is these issues that are discussed in this chapter.

GENERAL ASSUMPTION

The questions will be based on police topics or issues.

No questions will be based on police experiences or scenarios. The questions concern life in general, and you can answer them using your work, volunteer, social or educational experiences. This should give you every opportunity to reply to the questions in your own way. No particular experiences are considered more worthy than others. For example, an answer outlining a school or college experience would be assessed in the same way as one outlining a work-based activity. What is important is the answer's content: the skills a Police Community Support Officer needs can be transferred from non-police experiences and subsequently developed.

Important note: Some police forces hold additional interviews after the candidates have completed the Assessment Centre successfully. If the force you have applied to holds such interviews, contact the force for advice and assistance on the content and style of the interviews.

Your role during the interview

Unlike the interactive and written exercises, during the interview you are expected to be yourself: you are not required to play a role. It is important that, no matter what questions you are asked, you provide full and honest answers.

Do not take anything for granted. The questioner can only score what he or she hears. If it is not said, it cannot be scored – do not presume that the questioner will assume the obvious. If appropriate, you should explain your thought processes as well as your actions.

Briefing

Before the interview, you will be given a short briefing that outlines which room your interview will take place in and the structure it will follow. When you arrive in the interview room, the interviewer will read from a card an outline of what will happen during the interview. He or she will explain that you will be asked a series of questions and that the maximum time allowed to answer each question is five minutes. This would usually be timed by the interviewer using a stopwatch.

He or she will also explain that, if you answer in less than five minutes, you will move on to the next question. Any time not used in one question, however, cannot be added to the next: the maximum time for each of the four questions is always five minutes.

If you finish the interview early, you will usually be told to remain in the interview room until the other candidates have finished. This is because most Assessment Centres do not have a holding room in which you could wait until the other candidates finish. Should this happen, do not attempt to engage the interviewer in conversation – just sit quietly until you are told you may leave.

The structure of the interview

Normally, the only people in the room will be the interviewer and yourself. At the start of each five minutes, the interviewer states which competency area is being considered before he or she asks you the question. When you answer the question, the interviewer will assess your response.

Sometimes a third person may be present. This is to ensure that the questions are being asked and assessed appropriately. Should this happen, the reasons why this third person is there will be explained to you.

The interviewer will also have a number of prompts he or she can use to ask you to explain, or expand on your answers. If a question concerned team working, for example, a prompt might be as follows: 'Tell me what your role was in the team.' This prompt would encourage you to explain more about what you did in the team.

There may be five or six prompts for each question. If the interviewer does not need to use a particular prompt, he or she will not ask it. For example, if a candidate included a great deal of detail in his or her reply to the original team-working question (about what the team did, his or her role in it and how his or her role impacted on the rest of the team), asking the candidate what role he or she played in the team would not be appropriate.

Remember, the interviewer can only use the prescribed prompts, and they use them to help you achieve the best possible scores you can. Prompts are not there to try to catch you out.

You will be told at the start of the interview how many questions will be asked and that each question may have additional prompts. Your information pack will tell you how many questions you will be asked (usually four) and the competency area each question will cover.

GENERAL ASSUMPTION

Interviewers are looking to catch out or trip up candidates during questioning.

FACT

Interviewers use scripted additional prompts to question candidates in order for them to answer each question to the best of their ability.

One question, one competency

It has been mentioned on more than one occasion in this book that you should have a thorough understanding of what each competency area covers. This knowledge will help you to keep your answers focused on the appropriate indicators within that area.

TASK 1

Interview question

Below is a question with space for you to write the answer you would give in the interview. (If you prefer, ask someone to read the question to you and to note down your reply.) Also below are example prompts that could be used to encourage you to explain or develop your answers.

This question is in the competency area Team Working.

Please tell me about a time when you have worked as part of a team to complete a goal or task.

Prompt 1: Tell me what your role in the team was.

Prompt 2: Outline exactly what you did.

Prompt 3: Tell me how you helped or supported others in the team.

Prompt 4: How did you assist the team to get over any difficulties or obstructions in achieving the goal or task?

Prompt 5: What was the final outcome with regards to achieving the goal or task?

TASK 1	*continued*

Prompt 6: Is there anything else you wish to add in response to this question?

When you have completed this task, see how your answer compares with the Team Working competency area and its positive indicators. The assessor's checklist may not include all the positive indicators but it will include those appropriate to the question. Remember to consider not only which part of your answer relates to which indicators but also whether your answer provides strong or weak evidence.

While the interviewer will be concerned mainly with the stated competency area for each question, he or she will also assess your oral communication skills and Respect for Race and Diversity. Your oral communication skills are scored in the same way as they are for the interactive exercises. Any evidence you may give relating to other competency areas will not be assessed.

Before you attend for assessment, consider your past experiences and how you could use these to answer the questions. Practise answering possible questions, keeping your eye on the competency areas listed in **Appendix A**.

Example answer

An answer to prompt 3 may be as follows: 'Before starting the task we checked that everyone had the skills to do their part of the task and, if they didn't, we either arranged training or we moved them on to other roles.' This part of the answer covers the following indicators:

- Makes time to get to know people.
- Co-operates and supports others.
- Offers to help other people.
- Develops mutual trust and confidence in others.

The assessor would then make a decision about the strength of the answer. While it has merits, it only explains what was done at the start of the process. A fuller answer would go on to explain how support was provided throughout the activity. The answer is further weakened because the assessor would not be clear as to what the candidate actually did, as opposed to the team as a whole.

The assessor adds up how many indicators on his or her checklist for that question have been achieved and then decides how well each was done. A final grade for that question is then awarded.

Using the five minutes to best effect

Remember, you can score very well without saying everything you want to say about a particular question, so don't worry if you are stopped because the five minutes is up. If you are asked a question for which you cannot think of an answer, the interviewer will suggest you return to that question after you have answered the others. You will not be marked down for this, but neither will you be granted extra time for the same question being asked twice.

If you finish before the end of the five minutes, the questioner will always ask you a general prompt, similar to number 6 above. While you should not talk just for the sake of talking, you can only score when you are talking. The five minutes is yours and, if you have the time, it is worth recapping on your answers. There are two reasons for this:

- Working through an answer from the beginning to the conclusion can often prompt you to expand on, or explain part of your answer more fully.

- By repeating an answer you may score the same area again, but if you use different words or expand your answer, you may score that area more strongly than before. Your strongest answer is always used when calculating your final grade. Similarly, if you touch on the same area again and again, as long as each part of your answer adds to the evidence, this will be taken into consideration when the strength of your answer is assessed.

How the interview scores are used

The scores for each question are added to the scores you achieve for the same competency areas in the other exercises. This produces your total for that competency area. For example, one of the interview questions covered Community and Customer Focus. This was also covered in one interactive and one written exercise. These three scores are added together to produce your final score for this competency area. This score is then added to your overall assessment.

TOP TIPS

- Be prepared for a very structured interview.

- Before attending the Assessment Centre, consider in detail the competency areas the questions will be based on.

- Prepare answers in your mind that you may be able to use in the interview.

- Keep your answers focused on the stated competency area.

- Listen carefully to prompts and expand on, or add to your answer accordingly.

- Make sure you explain your involvement when you are asked about your previous experiences.

- Use your full five minutes for each question.

- Should you finish early, recap on your answer.

INDIVIDUAL LEARNING POINTS

_____

_____

_____

_____

_____

_____

_____

_____

_____

Chapter 8
Respect for Race and Diversity

Introduction

The task in **Chapter 2** will have shown you what this competency area is all about, but it is worth repeating here. Respect for Race and Diversity means to consider and show respect for the opinions, circumstances and feelings of colleagues and members of the public, no matter what their position, background, circumstances, status or appearance.

To achieve this competency area you must understand other people's views and take these into account. You must also be tactful and diplomatic when dealing with people, treating them with dignity and respect at all times. You must understand and be sensitive to social, cultural and racial differences. Although race and diversity are included in this area, it is not restricted to certain groups only. It is worth, therefore, revisiting **Appendix A** to review both the positive and negative indicators.

Why this area is important

Many inquiries and reports into the police service have shown that policing breaks down when the community it serves feels alienated from the police and their actions. The police service is built on the concept of 'policing by consent'. This concept is crucial if the public are to support the police in maintaining a safe and secure society. Indeed one of the reasons for the introduction of Police Community Support officers is to assist and make easier the contact the public are able to have with the police service.

The most recent and far-reaching investigation into how policing is conducted was the Stephen Lawrence Inquiry. This inquiry introduced the term 'institutional racism'. In simple terms, this means having policies and procedures – official or otherwise – that disadvantage certain racial or ethnic groups. The report of this inquiry had a dramatic impact on the police service, and it is one of the reasons why the police service use nationally recognised recruitment and promotion processes which can and are monitored and scrutinised.

The term 'institutional racism' can be broadened to include all sectors of society. Take, for example, a group of 'hoodies' standing at a street corner talking. Many people would assume that they are up to no good. Should Police Community Support Officers assume this, it would considerably affect any exchanges the Police Community Support Officers and youths had?

TASK 1

Considering Respect for Diversity

Local residents have complained about problems they have had with teenagers in their neighbourhood. You are one of two Police Community Support Officers officers who have been asked to patrol this area. You see a group of six youths standing on a street corner with hoods covering their heads and faces. They appear to turn away from you. Remember, you are there because of complaints from local residents, and these residents will be watching what you do.

Before continuing, list below the actions you would consider in these circumstances.

Having done this, review your responses against the indicators for this competency area (see **Appendix A**). First, identify those intended behaviours that would be considered positive. Now consider any actions or behaviours you would have done that would have gone against the indicators listed under Respect for Race and Diversity. For example if you considered just moving the youths on without talking to them first you certainly would not have been able to score the indicator 'listens to and values other's views and opinions'. (Remember, try to develop your skills so that only positive behaviours are observed during your assessment.)

Your opening comments to the group could dramatically affect their perception of the police: they may well have nothing to hide and are just standing there, talking. They only turned away because of their previous bad interactions with Police Community Support Officers. From their point of view they have done nothing wrong, and they are being picked on simply because of their dress code.

Should you just tell them bluntly to move on or they will be arrested, it would be easy to see why they have issues with the police. It would be much better if you told the group why you were in the area, mentioned the local residents' concerns and discussed with them why they congregate on street corners, etc.

Obviously, if it became apparent that the group were involved in anti-social or otherwise unlawful behaviour, then the exchange would be different. However, there is still a requirement even under these circumstances to treat people, as far as possible, with dignity and respect.

GENERAL ASSUMPTION

When 'older' people complain about teenagers, the 'older' people must be in the right and the teenagers in the wrong.

> **FACT**
>
> This may or may not be the case. If you are presented with a scenario like this at the Assessment Centre, consider the facts you have been given: what is fact and what is assumption?
>
> For example, a group of youths have been seen hanging around an area, and this has been recorded on CCTV cameras. The next morning, there is graffiti on the walls in this area. The local residents are up in arms and are convinced these youths caused the damage.
>
> From the information you have been given, this is an assumption. If at the Assessment Centre you were asked to speak to a local resident, first establish what is fact and what is assumption. If there is no evidence that the youths were responsible, you should make it clear that, while such damage is unacceptable, inquiries will have to be made to establish who was responsible and that action will be taken to prevent it from happening again.

Many candidates have opinions similar to the following:

- Groups of youths cannot be trusted.
- Youths wearing hoods have something to hide.
- The youth of today have little respect for property or people.
- If a group of youths is in an area and something happens, then they must be responsible.

Candidates with opinions such as these side easily with role actors who are playing the part of victims. Such candidates often say 'they shouldn't be allowed to wear hoods' or 'that behaviour is typical of young people today'. Comments like this do not display many of the positive indicators for Respect for Race and Diversity. They do not demonstrate:

- considering the issue from the teenagers' point of view;
- treating them with dignity and respect;
- tolerance;
- respect for their needs;
- understanding; or
- respect for their values as these fall within what is lawful.

At the Assessment Centre you must show appropriate respect to all groups at all times, even if a group is not physically present. Do not express commonly held, stereotypical views.

How the area is scored

As mentioned elsewhere in this book, Respect for Race and Diversity is assessed all the time you are at the Assessment Centre – and this includes arriving at or leaving the centre. For example, a candidate is seen to hit another car when he is reversing out of the car park at the end of the Assessment Centre. Instead of reporting this, he drives off. This candidate's behaviour demonstrates the following:

- He has clearly not shown respect for the circumstances and feelings of his colleagues.

- He has not treated the other car owner with respect.

- He has not identified and respected other people's values as these fall within what is lawful.

- He has not been open and honest.

- He has not considered the other car owner's feelings.

There are Respect for Race and Diversity evidence sheets to record inappropriate behaviour such as this. Anyone in the assessment team who witnesses such behaviour is required to record what he or she saw or heard on these sheets. He or she should describe – in as much detail as possible – what took place, using the candidate's own words if this is appropriate. Any other team members who witnessed the incident will also sign the sheet to confirm that they, too, observed this behaviour.

A panel will then review this sheet. If the candidate had been successful at the Assessment Centre, it would be up to the panel to make the decision as to the candidate's suitability for appointment.

If inappropriate behaviour is displayed during the interactive exercises, written exercises or interview, this will be scored on the relevant assessment sheet under the competency area Respect for Race and Diversity. The observed behaviour will also be recorded on the Respect for Race and Diversity evidence sheet. The grade normally awarded under such circumstances would be a D. The Assessment Centre manager and the panel will review this score, bearing in mind the evidence recorded on the sheet. If they uphold the D then, no matter what else the candidate has scored, he or she will fail the Assessment Centre.

It is impossible to give a list of comments that would be deemed inappropriate, but if candidates express views that are sexist, racist or homophobic, then, quite rightly, they would be unsuccessful. You should, therefore, think about this area carefully. Candidates who hold such views should not consider a career in the police service: Police Community Support Officers must remain impartial at all times, even when their own values would naturally cause them to be sympathetic to one view rather than another.

Interview questions

It is likely that one of the interview questions will be based on this competency area. If this is the case, you will be notified in advance via your information pack. It is worthwhile preparing yourself for such a question because this will give you the opportunity to think about your own values and behaviours carefully and honestly, and to compare these with the positive and negative indicators. It will also mean you will have examples ready for when you are questioned.

An example question for Respect for Race and Diversity is as follows: 'Please tell me about a time when you've amended your behaviour or language to take into account another person's views or values.' Remember, your answers do not have to relate just to race and diversity but may include any differences in society. Below are a few examples:

- Not using the expression 'Christ' because you work with Christians.

- When organising a Christmas party, you ensure that non-alcoholic drinks are available.

- When on holiday, you change what you wear to conform with local customs or requirements (i.e. not going topless).

- Introducing flexitime to allow people with childcare commitments to achieve a work–life balance.

- Even though you are permitted to play a radio quietly at work, you only play it when your boss is not there because she does not like people playing radios.

- Not mowing your lawn until mid-afternoon because your neighbour works nights and sleeps in the morning.

When answering, explain the differences between your own views and those of the other party, then describe how you considered and took into account their views and then amended your behaviour in the light of these differences.

The follow-up questions the interviewer could use may include the following:

- How did you become aware of this issue or problem?

- What did you consider before amending your thoughts or actions?

- What did you do about it?

- How do you feel about the other party's position?

- What was the resolution?

Remember, if there is time remaining you will be asked if you have anything further to add to your answer. Should you have time remaining in the 5 minutes use it to recap your answer.

GENERAL ASSUMPTION

If you are asked an interview question regarding this competency area, better answers relate to sexual orientation or issues related to colour or race.

FACT

Unless the question is specifically related to a stated issue then the answer could relate to any differences in society.

TOP TIPS

- Study the positive and negative indicators for Respect for Race and Diversity.

- Consider any behaviours that you usually display that if revealed during assessment would go against one or more of the stated indicators in this competency area.

- Remember that Respect for Race and Diversity relates to all differences in society.

- Use appropriate behaviour and language at all times.

- Deal with facts – do not make assumptions.

- During the exercises and tests, respect all the parties, even if they are not physically present.

- Do not stereotype.

- Remember, you are being observed even when you are not under formal assessment conditions.

- Bear in mind the positive indicators when you answer the Respect for Race and Diversity interview question.

INDIVIDUAL LEARNING POINTS

Chapter 9
After the Assessment Centre

Appeals

When you have completed the Assessment Centre, you are debriefed by the invigilators. The invigilators will tell you that you should raise any issues or concerns about the operation of the Assessment Centre before you leave the site. Any issues raised after the event will not be considered. You may discuss any concerns you have in private, away from the other candidates. You should not be afraid to highlight anything that may have adversely affected your performance, although it is rare for such things to happen.

Sometimes candidates say they knew a role actor or assessor personally and that this hindered their performance. While this is unfortunate, it is not grounds for appeal. Police Community Support Officers sometimes have to deal with people they consider to be their friends, but they still have to handle such situations in their professional capacity as a Police Community Support Officer. Everyday occurrences that may interrupt the running of the Assessment Centre, such as fire alarms, are normally remedied on the day by allowing the candidates extra time to finish. Such everyday occurrences are similarly not accepted as grounds for appeal.

Feedback on the assessment process

At the end of the assessment you will be given a questionnaire and a prepaid return envelope. This questionnaire asks you to comment on the appropriateness of the exercises and tests and to say whether you felt you were given the opportunity to demonstrate your skills and abilities to the full. The questionnaire is not part of the assessment process, and candidates are not monitored to see who completes and returns them. The comments the candidates make in the questionnaire are used to assess the effectiveness of the exercises and tests.

The assessors, role actors and members of the management team are also asked to comment on how well they felt the assessment went. The feedback obtained from all those involved consistently shows that the overwhelming majority believe the Assessment Centre is fair and appropriate (remember, some of these people are employees working within the police service).

Immediately after the Assessment Centre

The Assessment Centre is a demanding process, requiring concentration on your part over a long period of time. Take time to relax, therefore, once the assessment is over, particularly if you have to drive. If you have not eaten, have something to eat now. Also bear in mind that, even though the assessment has officially come to an end, you are still being observed and that any inappropriate behaviour will be recorded.

Fitness considerations

All police forces will require candidates to be examined or to complete a medical questionnaire. This may include a request asking for a candidate's permission to consult with the candidate's general practitioner. A lot of forces consider a candidate's body mass index when considering suitability for appointment. In simple terms this considers the fat of an individual. If this is an issue then attempt to correct this prior to your application being made. In addition to the above some forces will require candidates to be tested with regards to substance abuse. All forces will require candidates to complete an eyesight test or to obtain a report from their optician. It is recommended that if candidates have any concerns regarding their fitness or well-being that they discuss these with the force to which they have applied at the earliest opportunity either before or during the recruitment process.

Police force interviews

Police forces retain the right to require a candidate to complete an additional interview before or following the completion of the assessment centre. These interviews can be general or to clear up a particular point from your application or to clarify something that happened during the assessment centre. If the police force you have applied to holds such interviews, you will normally be notified of the time and location of your interview when you receive your assessment results.

If the interviews are general they will usually be of a formal nature and you will appear before a panel of three interviewers, one of whom is often a senior police officer. They last between 30 and 40 minutes and the questions you are asked normally concern that particular police force. Typical questions are as follows:

- Why do you want to be a Police Community Support Officer?

- What are the qualities you would bring to the role of a Police Community Support Officer?

- What are your hopes and aspirations for your chosen career?

- What are the main issues that concern this force?

- What are the objectives in the current policing plan?

You may also be asked questions about topical police or political issues, so it is a good idea to watch news programmes and to read the quality newspapers.

Because each force organises its own interviews, it is difficult to give specific advice about them. You should therefore ask the force how long it will last and who will be present. You could also inquire about the types of questions you will be asked – for example, whether about your previous experiences or whether about the force you have applied to. If they will ask you questions about the force itself, you should, as a minimum, obtain, read and understand that force's annual report.

Results from the Assessment Centre

The marks awarded to each candidate are sent to a central marking point. Although the exercises and interview questions are marked electronically, the marks are checked manually to make sure they are correct. The results are usually published within the next 14 days and they are sent to the relevant police forces. Each force then notifies its candidates in writing about their results.

You should not telephone in for your results as this slows the marking process down. It would also be unfair if candidates received their results at different times and through different methods.

Feedback

In addition to your results, some forces will also send detailed written feedback. Each individual force will have decided whether to provide feedback or not. Whether feedback is provided or not some candidates are annoyed with their results and immediately telephone for more information. Should you be disappointed with your results, and should feedback have been provided wait at least 24 hours before you read it. Whether feedback is provided or not it is always good practice to consider how you performed at assessment against the competencies, and then to consider that against feedback if provided.

Following receiving your results and any written feedback while there is nothing wrong in ringing for further information, remember that it is very unlikely the person you are speaking to was present at your assessment. Even if he or she was, it is highly improbable this person will remember you.

Should written feedback be provided it will relate to the exercises and the interview questions. This will outline which competency areas were being assessed, what grades you achieved and how well you performed in comparison with the other candidates. You are also sent a grid-like table with the competency areas down one side and the exercises across the top. This shows you the grades you were awarded for each exercise and the interview questions (remember, A is the top mark and D the bottom). This will tell you, at a glance, which competency areas you were strong in and which require work.

On seeing a poor mark in one competency area, some candidates often feel the assessment must have been flawed in some way. Should you feel this, revisit that competency area and look at the listed indicators within the competency area. Use your own recollections of the Assessment Centre and the written feedback to reflect honestly on your performance: which of the positive indicators did you not provide strong evidence for while you were being assessed?

An example grid is as follows:

	Exercise 1 'Collins'	Exercise 2 'Exercise Name'	Exercise 3 'Exercise Name'	Exercise 4 'Exercise Name'
Respect for Race and Diversity	C	B	B	B
Team Working		B	B	C
Community and Customer Focus	D		C	D
Effective Communication	A	B	B	B
Personal Responsibility		C	C	D
Resilience	C	B	C	B

This candidate scored well in the area of Effective Communication but poorly in Community and Customer Focus. His or her score for oral communication skills would be included in the score for Effective Communication.

In addition to this grid, you will be sent an outline of the exercises that explains what the exercises were about, what competency areas were being assessed and what you did well and not so well. An example outline using the interactive exercise 'Collins' from earlier in this book is as follows.

'Collins' Exercise

Binney Collins attended the hospital to visit a relative and while there her daughter became lost. She subsequently complained about the way the situation was handled. The candidates met with Collins to discuss what took place. The competency areas being assessed were Resilience; Community and Customer Focus; Effective Communication; and Respect for Race and Diversity.

You scored as follows:

Resilience	Grade C
Community and Customer Focus	Grade D
Effective Communication	Grade A
Respect for Race and Diversity	Grade C

Candidates who scored less strongly tended not to consider the lost person policy or to consider what had, or had not been done when viewed against the requirements of the policy. Candidates should reconsider the competency area(s) they scored poorly in – in this case, Community and Customer focus.

It is not possible to give candidates further detailed feedback as the exercises may still be in use.

Resitting the Assessment Centre

There is a national set time limit before candidates may resit the Assessment Centre. Currently this is six months but, if a candidate is unsuccessful in the competency area Respect for Race and Diversity, it is extended to 12 months. Failure in the competency area Respect for Race and Diversity can cause candidates to be told to wait longer before reapplying. Time limits for reapplication are changed periodically for a variety of reasons so always check the required time period before reapplication. The purpose of these time limits is to give candidates the opportunity to reflect on their performance and on the feedback they have received so that they may develop their skills.

Should a candidate have multiple applications into a number of Police Services (this is at the discretion of the Forces involved) the candidate would still only be allowed to sit one Assessment Centre within the prescribed time period. A pass from one Assessment Centre for one Police Service may be accepted by another; however, they would not allow this to be a method of candidates avoiding delays in recruiting.

Should you be unfortunate to be unsuccessful on your first Assessment Centre, do not consider any national limits for reapplication as the benchmark. Consider what you did and any feedback you received and then set about developing your skills accordingly, only reapplying when being totally confident that you understand and can meet the stated requirements. Numerous reapplications ending in similar results can allow forces to make the decision not to consider subsequent applications.

Using the feedback if you are successful

Following their appointment to a force, candidates are expected to use the feedback they received from the Assessment Centre to identify those competency areas that need developing during their initial training. Guided by their trainers, candidates will draw up action plans for those competency areas they are weak in.

Monitoring the Assessment Centre

The results from the Assessment Centre are constantly monitored, particularly with regard to candidates' sex, race, age and educational attainment. If it becomes apparent that a particular group is being unfairly disadvantaged, research will be undertaken to assess what is happening and why it is happening. Action will then be taken to remedy the situation.

TOP TIPS

- Raise any issues or concerns you may have regarding the Assessment Centre before you leave.

- Complete and return the candidate questionnaire.

- Try to relax for a while when you have completed the Assessment Centre, particularly before driving.

- Find out about and prepare for any other test.

- Should there be a second interview, ask the force about its structure and content and prepare accordingly.

- Take time to digest your results and any feedback you receive.

- Use this feedback, if received, in your action plans.

INDIVIDUAL LEARNING POINTS

_____

_____

_____

_____

_____

_____

_____

_____

_____

Appendix A
National Core Competencies

Reproduced in part from *The Integrated Competency Behavioural Framework – Version 9.0* (May 2007) by Skills for Justice

1 Competency Area: Respect for Race and Diversity

Considers and shows respect for the opinions, circumstances and feelings of colleagues and members of the public, no matter what their race, religion, position, background, circumstances, status or appearance.

Required level

Understands other people's views and takes them into account. Is tactful and diplomatic when dealing with people. Treats them with dignity and respect at all times. Understands and is sensitive to social, cultural and racial differences.

Positive indicators

- Sees issues from other people's viewpoints.
- Is polite, tolerant and patient with people inside and outide the organisation, treating them with respect and dignity.
- Shows understanding and sensitivity to people's problems and vulnerabilities.
- Respects the needs of eveyone involved when sorting out disagreements.
- Deals with diversity issues and gives positive, practical support to staff who may feel vulnerable.
- Listens to and values other's views and opionions.
- Uses language in an appropriate way and is sensitive to the way it may affect people.
- Acknowledges and respects a broad range of social and cultural customs, beliefs and values within the law.
- Understands what offends others and adapts own actions accordingly.
- Respects and maintains confidentiality, wherever appropriate.
- Delivers difficult messages sensitively.
- Challenges inappropriate attitudes, language and behaviour that is abusive, aggressive or discriminatory.
- Takes into account others' personal needs and interests.
- Supports minority groups both inside and outside their organisation.

Negative Indicators

- Does not consider other people's feelings.
- Does not encourage people to talk about personal issues.
- Criticises people without considering their feelings and motivation.
- Makes situations worse with inappropriate remarks, language or behaviour.
- Is thoughtless and tackless when dealing with people.
- Is dismissive and impatient with people.
- Does not respect confidentiality.
- Unneccessarily emphasises power and control in situations where this is not appropriate.
- Intimidates others in an aggressive and overpowering way.
- Uses humour inappropriately.
- Shows bias and prejudice when dealing with people.

2 Competency Area: Team Working

Develops strong working relationships inside and outside the team to achieve common goals. Breaks down barriers between groups and involves others in discussions and decisions.

Required level

Works effectively as a team member and helps build relationships within it. Actively helps and supports others to achieve team goals.

Positive indicators

- Understands own role in a team.
- Actively supports and assists the team to reach their objectives.
- Is approachable and friendly to others.
- Makes time to get to know people.
- Co-operates with and supports others.
- Offers to help other people.
- Asks for and accepts help when needed.
- Develops mutual trust and confidence in others.
- Willingly takes on unpopular or routine tasks.
- Contributes to team objectives no matter what the direct personal benefit may be.
- Acknowledges that there is often a need to be a member of more than one team.
- Takes pride in their team and promotes their team's performance to others.

Negative Indicators

- Does not volunteer to help other team members.
- Is only interested in taking part in high-profile and interesting activities.
- Takes credit or successes without recognising the contribution of others.
- Works to own agenda rather than contributing to team performance.
- Allows small exclusive groups of people to develop.
- Play one person off against another.
- Restricts and controls what information is shared.
- Does not let people say what they think.
- Does not offer advice or get advice from others.
- Shows little interest in working jointly with other groups to meet the goals of everyone involved.
- Does not discourage conflict within the organisation.

3 Competency Area: Community and Customer Focus

Focuses on the customer and provides a high-quality service that is tailored to meet their individual needs. Understands the communities that are served and shows an active commitment to policing that reflects their needs and concerns.

Required level

Provides a high level of service to customers. Maintains contact with customers, works out what they need and responds to them.

Positive indicators

- Presents an appropriate image to the public and other organisations.
- Supports strategies that aim to build an organisation that reflects the community it serves.
- Focuses on the customer in all activities.
- Tries to sort out customers' problems as quickly as possible.
- Apologises when they are at fault or have made mistakes.
- Responds quickly to customer requests.
- Makes sure that customers are satisfied with the service they receive.
- Manages customer expectations.
- Keeps customers updated on progress.
- Balances community and organisational interests.
- Sorts out errors or mistakes as quickly as possible.

Negative Indicators

- Is not customer-focused and does not consider individual needs.
- Does not tell customers what is going on.
- Presents an unprofessional image to customers.
- Only sees a situation from their own view, not from the customer's view.
- Shows little interest in the customer – only deals with their immediate problem.
- Does not respond to the needs of the local community.
- Slow to respond to customers' requests.
- Fails to check that customers' needs have been met.
- Focuses on organisational issues rather than customer needs.
- Does not make the most of opportunities to talk to people in the community.

4 Competency Area: Effective Communication

Communicates ideas and information effectively, both verbally and in writing. Uses language and a style of communication that is appropriate to the situation and people being addressed. Makes sure that others understand what is going on.

Required level

Speaks clearly and concisely, and does not use jargon. Uses plain English and correct grammar. Listens carefully to understand.

Positive indicators

- Makes sure all written and spoken communication is concise and well structured.
- Communicates information in a friendly and approachable style.
- Uses appropriate language and does not use jargon.
- Makes sure communication has a clear purpose.
- Makes sure communication is factual and accurate, and provided at the right time.
- Communicates information in an interesting way.
- Pays attention and shows interest in what others are saying.
- Uses correct spelling, punctuation and grammar.
- Listens carefully to understand.
- Asks questions to clarify issues.

Negative Indicators

- Is hesitant, nervous and uncertain when speaking.
- Speaks without first thinking through what to say.
- Uses inappropriate language or jargon.
- Speaks in a rambling way.
- Does not consider the target audience.

- Avoids answering difficult questions.
- Does not give full information without beng questioned.
- Writes in an unstructured way.
- Uses poor spelling, punctuation and grammar.
- Assumes others understand what has been said without actually checking.
- Does not listen and interrupts at inappropriate times.

5 Competency Area: Personal Responsibility

Takes personal responsibility for making things happen and achieving results. Displays motivation, commitment, perseverance and conscientiousness. Acts with a high degree of integrity.

Required level

Takes personal responsibility for own actions and for sorting out issues or problems that arise. Is focused on achieving results to required standards and developing skills and knowledge.

Positive indicators

- Accepts personal responsibility for own decisions and actions.
- Displays initiative, taking on tasks without having to be asked.
- Takes action to resolve problems and fulfil own responsibilities.
- Keeps promises and does not let colleagues down.
- Takes pride in own work
- Is conscientious in completing work on time.
- Follows things through to a satisfactory conclusion.
- Self-motivated, showing enthusiasm and dedication to their role.
- Focuses on a task even if it is routine.
- Improves own professional knowledge and keeps it up to date.
- Is open, honest and genuine, standing up for what is right.
- Makes decisions based upon ethical considerations and organisational integrity.
- Aware of their own strengths and weaknesses.

Negative Indicators

- Passes responsibility upwards inappropriately.
- Is not concerned about letting others down.
- Will not deal with issues, just hopes they will go away.
- Blames other rather than admitting to mistakes or looking for help.
- Unwilling to take on responsibility.
- Puts in the minimum effort that is needed to get by.
- Shows a negative and disruptive attitude.

- Shows little energy or enthusiasm for work.
- Expresses a cynical attitude to the organisation and their job.
- Gives up easily when faced with problems.
- Fails to recognise personal weaknesses and development needs.
- Makes little or not attempt to develop self or keep up to date.

6 Competency Area: Resilience

Shows resilience, even in difficult circumstances. Prepared to make difficult decisions and has the confidence to see them through.

Required level

Shows confidence to perform own role without unnecessary support in normal circumstances. Acts in an appropriate way and controls emotions.

Positive indicators

- Deals confidently with members of the public, drawing on skills and experience.
- Is comfortable working alone with an appropriate level of supervision and guidance.
- Puts a positive view on situations and concentrates on what can be achieved.
- Is aware of and manages personal stress.
- Accepts criticism and praise.
- Controls emotions and does not get emotionally involved in disputes.
- Is patient when dealing with people who make complaints.
- Acts in a confident way when challenged.
- Says 'no' when necessary.
- Takes a rational and consistent approach to work.

Negative Indicators

- Gets easily upset, frustrated and annoyed.
- Panics and becomes agitated when problems arise.
- Walks away from confrontation when it would be more appropriate to get involved.
- Needs constant reassurance, support and supervision.
- Uses inappropriate physical force.
- Gets too emotionally involved in situations.
- Reacts inappropriately when faced with rude or abusive people.
- Deals with situations aggressively.
- Complains and whinges about problems rather than dealing with them.
- Gives in inappropriately when under pressure.
- Worries about making mistakes and avoids difficult situations wherever possible.

Appendix B
National Core Competencies: Checklist

Respect for Race and Diversity

Strengths

Areas for development

Team Working

Strengths

Areas for development

Community and Customer Focus

Strengths

Areas for development

Effective Communication

Strengths

Areas for development

Personal Responsibility

> *Strengths*

> *Areas for development*

Resilience

> *Strengths*

> *Areas for development*

Appendix C

Central Hospital Trust: Information Pack

Central Hospital Trust

Welcome.

We are delighted that you have been appointed as a Mobile First Contact Support Officer in the Central Hospital Trust. We hope you will find the job interesting, challenging and rewarding.

You will be formally introduced to the Trust's policies and procedures through a set training process. However, we have found that new staff have found the enclosed information useful.

We hope this will assist you to settle into your new job and would ask that you take time to read and digest the contents.

The following information is included:

- An overview of the Central Hospital Trust
- Mobile First Contact Support Officer's job description
- Patient Confidentiality Policy
- Equality Policy
- Parking Policy
- Lost Person Policy

Central Hospital Trust

Overview of the Central Hospital Trust

What we do

The Central Hospital Trust is proud to provide 24-hour, 365 days a year emergency medical care to the immediate and surrounding area. In addition to the emergency provisions, it provides outpatient appointments, maternity care and planned medical procedures. The Trust also provides for minor local procedures to be completed in GPs' surgeries or at temporarily identified accommodation if demand requires it.

How to get here

The Central Hospital Trust is well catered for in terms of regular bus and train services. In addition to public transport there is parking for 1,500 private cars. Parking provision and enforcement are subcontracted to an independent management company. To assist elderly patients the hospital provides a 'Friends of Central Trust Travel Service'. This is where volunteers provide a free private car service to patients who have no other form of transport.

Other facilities

To support staff and patients, an area of the Trust has been given over for shops to provide food, stationery and other items. There are ten outlets in total, all managed by independent companies. The retail outlets are not only used by the hospital population but also by residents local to the area. They operate between the hours of 8.00 am and 10.00 pm.

No smoking

The Trust is now no-smoking both inside buildings and anywhere outside within the Trust's boundaries. All staff should enforce this policy by politely asking patients and visitors to stop should they see the policy being broken.

Mobile First Contact Support Officers

Mobile First Contact Support Officers patrol the hospital buildings and grounds to provide support to visitors, staff and patients as required with non-medical issues or concerns. They also provide cover at fixed points to wards and departments, in the absence of First Contact Officers who are usually present at these areas.

Ward Managers or Matrons will deal with all medical issues or concerns in the first instance.

Refreshments for staff

In addition to the independent food retailers, the hospital provides a subsidised restaurant that operates on a 24-hour basis. This is only available to hospital staff or to the Friends of Central Trust Travel Service.

Mobile First Contact Support Officer's Job Description

Mobile First Contact Support Officers work at fixed points within the hospital and also patrol the hospital's buildings and grounds. Both of these duties are under the guidance and direction of their appointed First Contact Officer.

Times at fixed points, which will usually be at entrances to wards and departments, will be to cover for absences of First Contact Officers. This should be kept to a minimum.

Patrol by Mobile First Contact Support Officers can be self directed or targeted to observe and deal with issues as identified by their First Contact Officer.

The duty times will be agreed to ensure cover between 8.00 am and 10.00 pm.

Their main responsibilities under the direction of their First Contact Officer will be as follows:

- To act as a point of contact for all non medical issues for patients and visitors
- To receive, enquire into and resolve any concerns, non medical, from staff, patients or visitors
- To complete written reports on all matters reported to them
- To ensure the Patient Confidentiality Policy is adhered to and explained fully to patients and visitors when required. They will also be available to give staff advice on this issue
- To enforce, as required, the no smoking policy with staff, patients and visitors
- To give advice to staff, patients and visitors on the Equality Policy
- To assist First Contact Officer's in ensuring all Trust policies and procedures are complied with
- To work with the parking and shop managers regarding security and provision of services
- To provide assistance, as required, following the activation of fire or security alarms
- To deal, in the first instance, with non-hospital related issues such as lost children or drunk and abusive patients or visitors
- To ensure the free flow of traffic around the roads within the hospital complex.

Central Hospital Trust
Patient Confidentiality Policy

This Policy applies to all staff.

A duty of confidence arises when one person discloses information to another, where it is reasonable to expect that information will be held in confidence. This relates to all information about or provided by patients.

The general assumption must always be that information about or provided by patients is confidential and should not be used or disclosed in a form that might identify a patient without his or her consent.

The exception to this is where the patient has been notified on admissions (which is standard practice) that information associated with his or her health care will be shared, as required, within the medical environment for his or her benefit. In these cases, explicit consent is not required.

Prior to admission, patients will be asked to nominate an identified person whom the hospital can update following operations or procedures.

The patient and nominated person will have been advised that, once the hospital has updated the nominated person following the operation or procedure, any further callers to the hospital will be directed to him or her.

The patient and identified person will have agreed in advance as to whom and what information should be disclosed.

Central Hospital Trust

Equality Policy

It is intended that all staff, patients and visitors should follow this Policy. This Policy requires that no one on the hospital premises should receive less favourable treatment or be discriminated against because of:

- Gender
- Marital status
- Religion
- Political opinion
- Race
- Sexual orientation
- Disability
- Age
- Gender reassignment
- Nationality.

All Trust employees should note and challenge behaviour that is in breach of this Policy. Should they not be able to do so or should it be considered inappropriate to challenge the behaviour at that time, it should be reported to their Line Manager.

This relates to both employment opportunities and the health services provided by the Trust.

Discrimination includes harassment, which means unwelcome or unwanted behaviour.

Any such behaviour is totally unacceptable.

Anyone who feels they are being treated unfairly or without respect should take action. The following are suggestions, although this is not an exhaustive list:

1 Tell the person to stop (they may not know they are behaving inappropriately).

2 Talk to someone else, a manager or friend. They may be able to offer advice or assistance in seeking a resolution. A First Contact Officer/Mobile First Contact Support Officer will always be a point of contact and will be independent.

3 Make a formal complaint. This should be made in writing to the First Contact Manager.

The Policy seeks to ensure that legislation and the Trust's Policy are complied with and to ensure that everyone is treated with respect and dignity.

Central Hospital Trust

Parking Policy

Parking in the hospital environment is managed and enforced by an independent management company. This is for staff, patients and visitors' private vehicles.

Staff are able to park free of charge providing vehicles are correctly parked in staff-designated zones and vehicles are displaying the appropriate hospital vehicle passes.

All drivers of private vehicles are required to pay the charges for parking as indicated on the prominently displayed boards at the entrance to each car park.

The only exception to this are the 20-minute zones near to the entrances of each ward that allow for free short-term parking for the 'dropping off' and 'picking up' of patients.

Failure to park correctly or pay appropriate charges can lead to the award of a fixed penalty charge against the driver by the management company, who can subsequently enforce any non-payment as a civil debt.

Central Hospital Trust

Lost Person Policy

Patients can be lost for a variety of reasons and visitors to the hospital can often be emotional for a variety of reasons and should they have care of children it is easy for them to allow the children to walk away.

Experience has shown that once adults or children become lost they can rapidly reach all parts of the hospital's buildings or grounds, or even leave the premises totally.

Should an adult or child be reported missing either by a member of staff or a member of the public then a Mobile First Contact Support Officer should attend immediately and take the following actions: -

- Notify the Police
- Identify to the Police a fixed point of contact for them to attend at the hospital to take control
- Commence a written log of any actions taken
- Get a description of the missing adult or child
- Circulate the information to First Contact Officers for onward distribution to their respective Mobile First Contact Support Officers
- If a member of the public reported the missing person ensure that someone remains with them until the police are in attendance
- Conduct an immediate search of the area from where the adult or child was last seen
- Be present when the Police attend and provide any help and assistance as requested by the Police

This should not be considered an exhaustive list and any other actions, in addition to the above, should be taken if considered appropriate at the time.

Index